GEMSTONES
AND MINERALS

GEMSTONES AND MINERALS

A Guide for the Amateur Collector and Cutter

Paul Villiard

With Photographs by the Author

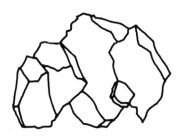

Winchester Press

To Edward Van Gaasbeek
lapidary and ardent rockhound
this book is dedicated in friendship and respect.

Book design and part title drawings by M. F. Gazze

Copyright © 1974 by Paul Villiard

Library of Congress Catalog Card Number: 73-78835

ISBN: 0-87691-139-4

Published by Winchester Press
460 Park Avenue, New York 10022

Printed in the United States of America

Contents

Preface

The collecting of rocks and minerals has interested people almost since the beginning of history. The Egyptians are known not only to have collected specimens of the natural rocks in which the earth abounds, but to have done some crude gem cutting and polishing as well.

The Aztecs and Incas also cut and polished stones and, like the Egyptians, drilled holes in them so they could be strung as crude necklaces. The marvel is not that they knew about working stones, but that they were able to do this with the crude and primitive tools and materials they had to work with. In order to drill a bead, for example, they used a bird quill and fine sand as an abrasive. Today, with our modern and efficient diamond drills, it sometimes takes one to three or four hours to drill through a piece of hard gem material. With a bird quill and sand, it took those ancient craftsmen days, and even weeks of constant work to achieve the same result!

A very creditable polish was obtained by those patient workmen, rubbing the stones by hand with fine sand, pumice taken from crushed lava rock, and other abrasives. Even with modern synthetic materials it takes a considerable amount of time and effort to cut and polish a stone.

Small wonder, then, that in the days of the Pharaohs and the Inca kings, jewelry was worn only by the very rich—the priesthood or the nobility—especially if it contained cut or polished gemstones.

Just a few years ago the art of working rocks and minerals into gemstones was confined to a comparatively few persons—specialists in what was practically a secret craft. The average person did not know the various steps necessary to produce a beautiful jewel. Also, machinery and equipment for gem cutting was very limited and difficult to purchase. Not many dealers carried such specialized equipment, and not knowing much about the processes involved, the amateur was usually unable to make it for himself.

In recent years, however, all this has changed. With the advent of the sintering process, whereby diamond powder could be sintered into wheels, discs, and even flexible cloth belts, the whole world of gem cutting was suddenly opened up to the hundreds of thousands of persons interested in working the seemingly intractable materials of the mineral world.

As soon as the diamond tools were made available, companies sprang up all over the country to manufacture tools and machines. Diamond saws, sanding machines, lapping discs, carving tools—all were now within reach of the amateur.

It is axiomatic that the amateur craftsman performs the major part in the development of any craft. He is the one who uses the machine, and he is the one who wants to make the process as easy as possible for producing the end product. Hence, he is the one who irons the "bugs" out of machines as they are invented, if indeed he does not do the actual inventing himself.

Every year now sees either the development of new tools and equipment for the working of gem material or the improvement of existing equipment. We are in the halcyon days of the craft, and can now take advantage of the almost unlimited supply of things to make out of small pieces of this earth.

Before we proceed, it might be a good idea to tell you just what the difference is between a rock and a mineral. A very simple comparison is this: A rock is a building, and a mineral is the bricks from which the building is made. Minerals are the basic ingredients which make up the composition of rocks. A rock, therefore, may be composed of several minerals, but the mineral is pure. There is a further breakdown, but one not visible to the naked eye: minerals are composed of many *elements*, rocks are composed of many *minerals*. Gemstones are cut from either minerals or rocks. Both minerals and rocks are collected as specimens.

About This Book

The purpose of this book is manyfold. There are innumerable publications available dealing with the many different aspects of "rockhounding," mineral collecting, specimen identification, gem cutting, and jewelry making. Literally dozens of pamphlets or books have been written, telling the reader where to look for material on field trips. Magazines have published lists of rock shops and collecting sites. In short, a person can spend months, or even years, riffling through all the printed material on this most popular subject in order to learn its various aspects.

But not everyone who would like to join the millions of interested "rockhounds" is able to perform this research. Not all have access to a great majority of these publications, nor would they know where to look for them.

The main purpose of this book, then, is to bring together enough of the information so that the reader will have a guide in whatever branch of the hobby he or she wishes to pursue.

Is your interest mainly in collecting minerals? One entire section is devoted to the identification and general location of over 100 different species. They all have their specific gravities, their hardness, their color, and their surface appearance listed for you, together with other salient features to enable you to recognize them when you see them, as well as the states in which they are found.

Would you like to spend your vacation on a field trip to known collecting sites, where you are practically guaranteed that you will find the material you want? Another section is devoted to the listing of fee-collecting sites, with detailed instructions as to how to get there by car.

And after you have your minerals, what would you like to do with them? Display them as specimens? You will find directions on how to prepare and display them. Cut them into gemstones? In Part II of this book, you will learn how to cut gemstones out of rough material, how to polish stones, how to work with opals and other more precious stones, and how to make rings, bracelets, spheres, and beads from your gems.

What tools and equipment do you need for gem cutting, and where do you get them? I have listed a number of companies and manufacturers who supply suitable equipment, machines, and tools. Every gem-making tool or machine mentioned in this book has been tested by me, and I have found those listed to work easily and well. So you may acquire any of them for your own use with the assurance that they are practical and easy to operate.

As an appendix, I have provided lists of books and periodicals that will take you further into collecting and gem making. There is also a short glossary of terms you will run across in this book and as you pursue your interest. Thus if you want to read selected chapters before you read the whole book straight through, you will be able to learn the meanings of terms that were discussed in chapters you have missed. Finally, there is a concise index so that the book can be a permanent reference.

About the only thing left out of this comprehensive book is the cutting of faceted stones. The reason is that this is an entire art in itself, and it is my intention to produce a companion volume in the near future that deals with this art exclusively.

Join, then, the ever-growing legion of persons who have discovered the rare and wonderful world of minerals and gemstones. The number at the time of this writing is close to ten million in this country alone! Certainly by the time you read these words, there will be still more, and I hope you will be one of them.

I
COLLECTING ROCKS AND MINERALS

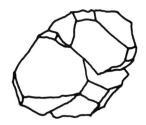

1.

How Rocks
and Minerals Are Formed

This planet, while it seems gigantic, solid, and rock-steady to the feeble and transient beings who populate its surface, is in reality the merest speck in the universe which surrounds it. The amazing thing about it is that it is so varied in construction.

During the formation of the planet itself, cataclysmic forces kept it in almost constant turmoil, with continents splitting open, then crashing shut once again. Volcanoes erupted, blasting the inner molten contents of the birthing globe to the heavens with a roar that must have been, if there had been ears to hear, truly deafening. Lakes — yes, even oceans — of rock, so superhot as to be liquid, seethed and boiled to the surface, cooling gradually, then breaking up into soil.

Out of this cooling magma, crystals of the different minerals congealed and grew, some or most of them deeply buried, either in the solidified rock inside which they formed, or in the rock ground into soil. Deposits formed to remain hidden until man finally discovered how to seek them out and mine them.

We speak of cataclysmic forces involved, but they really were not "cataclysmic" as we understand the word, since by definition a cataclysm is a sudden force or explosion, and there was nothing sudden about the forming of the earth and the minerals within it. True, a volcanic eruption can be geologically sudden, but that is all.

When we speak of a crystal "growing" in the earth, we are speaking of a period of *millions of years*. When we mention the pressure needed to form a mineral specimen — measured in thousands of tons, perhaps — we must also take into consideration that enormous span of time over which the pressure is distributed. It is not a sudden thing, the formation of a cluster of beautiful quartz crystals, or the crystalline lining of a geode. This covers a period of time so long that to us it is a meaningless number. A million years. Ten million years. A hundred million years. Each of these time units means nothing to you or me as we read them. A million years is hardly less than a hundred million years, nor is the latter much longer than the former. Yet, if you sit down and seriously and patiently try to conceive of that length of time, the mind bogs down in a fog of helplessness. The human mind simply cannot accept such a span. The human mind cannot even accept a span of one hundred years without the time becoming almost meaningless. And yet, one hundred years is so infinitesimally small in geological time that in the formation of a crystal, for example, it cannot be measured.

On the other hand, the formation of certain kinds of crystals may take place in an extremely short period of time. More about this phenomenon a little later on in this chapter.

Since it takes many thousands of years for most crystals to form, the pressures they are subjected to are also spread out over the same period of time. At any given moment the pressure is so slight as to be almost nonexistent. It is there, however. Have you ever seen a blade of grass growing right up through a paved driveway or road? Have you ever wondered how so slender and tender an object can exert sufficient pressure to push aside pavement and grow out into the sunlight? The same principle applies as that of being able to tow a huge ocean liner with a length of sewing thread, given the correct set of factors. With wind and wave abated, all you have to do is put tension on the thread to within the breaking point, and maintain that pressure. Eventually, the mass of the huge liner will move to relieve the pressure.

A cluster of "Herkimer diamonds," actually doubly terminated quartz crystals, shown in the matrix rock. A good cabinet specimen.

So the blade of grass applies the tiniest bit of pressure to the pavement, maintaining it constantly, until finally the pavement parts to give way before the pressure. So the crystal swells inside the rock as the materials which make it gradually collect under the growth. Slowly the rock gives way before the steady, relentless pressure—measured, perhaps, in billionths of ounces.

As a boy, I was always fascinated to see a mineral crystal growing inside a piece of its matrix rock. I could not conceive of that crystal forcing itself through the unyielding substance sur-

Twinned crystals of selenite growing through each other.

rounding it. I could not understand how each crystal of the same mineral could *grow* in exactly the same shape. On occasion I would be shown a twinned crystal, one penetrating right through another of the same kind. Well, this was one of those mysteries which were simply incapable of ever being solved by man! This same, slow application of pressure accounts for it.

One of the great mysteries to me, then, was how a rock—a hard, solid, intact rock—could be seen through. I spent most of my youth in the Pacific Northwest, where nearly every other pebble you picked up was an agate of some kind. When gleaning the streams or beaches for pretty pebbles, I noticed that the agates, when still wet, were transparent—some of them as clear as glass. When they dried off, the surface was opaque from the abrasion of the stream bed or beach, and I used to spend hours with my hoard of stones, wetting them to see which ones I could look down into.

Rocks have certain properties which make life on this planet possible. As a matter of fact, if it were not for these properties, life would never have evolved at all. Rocks possess attraction for everything else. This attraction, probably magnetic in property, we call gravity. Weight and gravity are sometimes thought of as being synonymous. We know some rocks are very heavy, while others are very light. The heavy ones have a greater attraction than the lighter ones, both of them possessing the same property in different degree.

It is the fact, however, that rocks are rigid and stiff that makes it possible for our planet to maintain its shape. If rocks were plastic like clay, for example, the rotation of the earth would in time force the globe to expand at the equator until the shape of the planet became disc-like, thicker in the middle and thin at the edges where the greatest spinning force was applied.

As stiff and unyielding as rocks are, they still can be bent, and this property enables the crust of the earth to move slowly without breaking open with each strain and stress application. If it were not for this plasticity, the earth would break up into smaller components and probably remain as merely a gathered mass of broken fragments. Examples of this bending property can be seen along road cuts, especially newer cuts which expose the layers of differently colored rock before they are covered with soil and plant growth.

Next, rocks break up and fragment, grinding first into pebbles, then sand, and finally soil. Soil builds up approximately one inch in a hundred years, and the gradual process is, at least partly, the result of fracturing due to freezing and thawing over the centuries. This alternate cold and heat causes the rocks to break into small chunks, and wind, water, and earth movement grinds them further into the fine soil. Chemical action also plays an important role.

Beaches are composed of sand, broken down from rocks that have been pounded apart over millenniums. A wonderful gradation of this water action may be observed if you travel from the coast of Maine, where the rocky shores are still covered with huge masses of unbroken rock, to the western shore of Lake

These two pictures show a complete wave in sedimentary rocks. The convex and concave parts of the wave are separated by about 300 feet. They could be separated by many miles, and still be part of the same upheaval that caused the rocks to bend.

Superior, where you will find long stretches of beach covered with wonderfully rounded rocks, from fist size to the size of your head. From here, go to the beaches of Oregon and Washington, where there are miles of pebble beaches having no stone larger than a walnut. Now the pleasure beaches of lower California are covered with fine, smooth sand, pleasant to run over in your bare feet.

Rocks are divided into three main classifications, although some geologists use four classifications: *igneous* rocks, *sedimentary* rocks, *metamorphic* rocks, and the fourth classification, *plutonic* rocks. Plutonic and igneous rocks are really the same classification, as we shall see, but occur in different ways.

Left: *Beaches of waterworn rocks often yield some treasures. Wetting the area will help detect gem minerals.*

Right: *Collecting agates at the wrack line on Agate Beach, Oregon.*

Igneous Rocks

Igneous rocks are simply rocks that were cast up during volcanic eruption and have cooled rapidly. Plutonic rocks are, equally simply, rocks which, while molten, were trapped beneath the surface and cooled much more slowly. Both igneous and plutonic rocks, therefore, were molten in their beginning.

If you have ever watched the eruption of a volcano or seen one in the movies or on television, you have watched igneous rock being formed. Molten rock deep beneath the surface of the earth is called *magma*, and this exists in enormous pools inside the earth's crust. When this magma seeps to the surface through vents, or is forced through a weak spot, as in a volcanic eruption, the molten rock flows over the surface, solidifying as lava. This is called *extrusive* igneous rock.

Sometimes the magma never reaches the surface, but solidifies far beneath the earth, filling huge vaults with solid masses of hardened rock. This is called *intrusive* igneous rock. Intrusive rock often fills a void, pushing up the rock on top of the cavity into a hill. These deposits are called *batholiths* and *laccoliths*. When the magma forces its way into a vertical crack in the existing rock, it is called a *dike*. The rocks above a batholith are bent into curves and waves, and sometimes these bent layers are exposed when a road is cut through the area, or by some other natural upheaval. If the void being filled with intrusive magma is horizontal between layers of existing rock, these deposits are called *sills*.

In the magma forming igneous rocks, the atoms are free when the temperature is high enough. These free atoms are of different sizes and different electrical charges—that is to say, both positive and negative charge—and they slowly migrate through the magma while it is still molten.

The magma can remain in its molten state over an immense period of time—anywhere from one million years to ten or a hundred million years, during which time the atoms are constantly migrating to form crystals of different minerals.

Those minerals having the lowest freeze point—that point at which the mineral is no longer fluid—form their crystals first, using the atoms that make up their structure as available. Minerals having higher freeze points follow according to the temperature drop of the magma, and according to the availability of their atoms. Naturally, if the first crystals formed used up all the available atoms of one element or another, it stands to reason that the next mineral would not be able to crystallize out if it, too, needed the same atoms.

Sometimes a layer of another mineral will block the migration of the atoms, taking them up for its own use, with the result that in some places you will have a layer rich in minerals, while directly above or below will be a layer deficient in mineral deposits. As the melt begins to cool and solidify there is a retarding effect on the movement of the atoms making up the crystals of the different minerals.

Also, layers below a certain level in the melt are usually very rich in minerals. In basalt, olivine atoms which are heavier than other atoms settle to the lower levels to form layers rich in olivine crystals, while throughout the rest of the melt the olivine crystals are smaller and much scattered. Thus you find centers where vast accumulations of crystals are to be found.

There are various kinds of melts. In a magma there are very rich hydrothermal deposits where certain minerals are carried out in solution. Hydrothermal deposits are superheated water under such enormous pressure that it remains liquid and does not turn into steam. This water, so superheated, has the ability to dissolve minerals until it becomes a supersaturated solution, migrating or seeping through the magma in veins, where the minerals are formed in rich deposits.

Pumice is an igneous lava that, while in the molten stage, has gases trapped in it to make it flow as a froth. Obsidian, when very old, will become porous and absorb water; then, when this mass is heated, it swells up into a similar froth. This substance is sold as *perlite*. Obsidian itself is an igneous rock that cooled so rapidly that the atoms had no time to arrange themselves into their regular crystalline habit. Consequently, obsidian is grainless and has a conchoidal fracture, a hard, lustrous surface, and polishes to an extremely glossy, liquid finish. Some obsidians are translucent, others opaque.

Sedimentary Rocks

Sedimentary rocks are, as the name implies, rocks formed from sediments. When sedimentary rock is found, that region was at one time a lake bottom or an ocean bed. The silts and mud, settling to the bottom, gradually hardened into rock in layers, sometimes of different colors and hardness, depending upon what minerals and foreign substances were present during that age when a layer was deposited. Shale and slate are common forms of sedimentary rocks. In the southwestern part of this country are deposits of sedimentary rocks so filled with small fossil shells as to be almost solid shell material. This rock is called *turitella,* after the name of the shells making up the rock.

Sedimentary rocks are almost entirely on the surface of the earth. Streams, rivers, and oceans have been depositing sedimentary layers throughout time. The Mississippi River, for example, has been flowing for over half a million years, and has been depositing silt and sediments for that entire period. The sedimentary layer from this river is now said to be over four miles thick!

Sedimentary rocks are quite variable in their layers. Some layers are thick; others are thinner. This is due to weather conditions as well as to the hardness of the rocks being disintegrated to form the silt. The riverbed, composed of rock, is constantly being worn down and the sediments carried to the delta to be dumped there. During periods of heavy rains, surface soils are washed into the river to be carried down with the rest of the silt. Pebbles and small rocks may also be washed into the flooding water to be tumbled on their way, worn down by the tumbling action and made smaller. Next may follow an age of drought, during which very little dirt or matter is carried downstream, resulting in a much thinner layer in the rock. Ages of heavy marine life will leave the remains of countless millions of an-

A piece of breccia. This one is made of fragmented jasper cemented with calcite and chalcedony.

imals, shells, and marine plants to form layers of varying thickness. Usually these layers are of different colors too, and in the Painted Desert one can see the brilliantly colored layers boldly standing out where the erosion of wind and water has exposed them to view.

Besides shale and slate, sedimentary rocks are limestone, sandstone, chalk, coal, gypsum, and conglomerate. Conglomerate results when rocks are tumbled down and left as a layer of rounded, water-worn pieces which later are cemented together into rock. Another form of rock made up of fragments cemented together is breccia. Breccia is exactly like conglomerate, except that the small rocks cemented together are broken fragments with

A layer of shale. A sedimentary rock filled with imprints of fossil shells. Ferns, fish, insects, and other prehistoric fossils are often found in stone layers.

sharp edges instead of water-worn rocks. Puddingstone is a form of breccia.

Halite is another form of sedimentary rock, better known as common salt. Deposits of halite miles thick are to be found in several places on earth. This is mined, purified, ground into fine particles, and used for table salt and for industrial purposes.

Sedimentary rocks are rich in fossils of many kinds. In limestone beds and in shales and slate deposits are to be found fossils of fishes, ferns, and other plants, as well as small animals. Important records of ancient life are to be taken from the layers of sedimentary rock from all over the world. Sulphur and iron are often present in shale in the form of iron pyrites, sometimes called "fool's gold." This crystallizes in the form of cubic shapes, often growing through each other in a marvelous cluster and making specimens of striking beauty.

Metamorphic Rocks

Metamorphic rocks are rocks which have been changed, or altered in composition. The changes which take place in metamorphic rocks are related to pressure, temperature, and chemical attack. This is to say that if the rock is changed due to pressure and temperature, it is remelted, permitting the atoms to move about and migrate to form new crystals. Sometimes these are merely the same minerals, but in higher concentration, thus making larger crystals. Sometimes they are entirely new minerals.

Thus, if granite, a slow-cooling igneous rock, became a metamorphic rock through remelt, the diminutive crystals of quartz could coalesce and form huge quartz crystals weighing many tons each.

Chemical attack can also cause a mineral to metamorphose into another mineral. Such minerals are interesting to note. A

The action of lichen on rocks returns the rocks to soil. The lichen makes acid which breaks down the rock into rich dirt, renewing the surface of the earth constantly.

deposit or crystal of one mineral may have its atoms exchanged, over a period of millenniums, for the atoms of another mineral. However, the changed crystal still maintains the shape of the original mineral, so we find a crystal of one mineral in the shape of another mineral, possibly in another crystalline group. Such minerals are called *pseudomorphs*.

So-called petrified wood is an example of atom exchange, although in this case the exchange was made of atoms of a living material being exchanged for atoms of a mineral. This simply means that there really is no such thing as petrified *wood*, since the material is no longer wood, but opal, agate, or quartz in one form or another which, in metamorphosing the wood, retained the shape, cell structure, and characteristics of the wood in wonderfully colored minerals. There are a great many different kinds of pseudomorphs after wood, and these can be very accurately identified, since the wood characteristics remain and can be studied under magnification. Some "petrified" woods are among the most colorful of all minerals, and can be cut into beautiful gemstones.

The earth's matter, as we know, is composed of over one hundred elements. It is a source of some amazement to many persons when they discover that 99.75% of the earth's crust is made up of only fifteen of these elements, leaving a mere 0.25% for *all other elements*. Within this tiny fraction of the crust are such things as gold, silver, copper, and other metals, as well as everything that is not included in the fifteen elements, which are:

Oxygen	Silicon	Aluminum	Calcium	Sodium
Potassium	Magnesium	Titanium	Phosphorus	Carbon
Hydrogen	Manganese	Sulphur	Chlorine	Iron

The crust of the earth's lithosphere is very much lighter than the core. This is partly due to the fact that three of the elements which make up the crust are gases — namely, oxygen, hydrogen, and chlorine. The heavier elements, such as nickel and iron, are mainly in the core. While iron is listed as one of the fifteen crust elements, the amount found in the crust is very small compared with the amount found in the core: somewhere on the order of 5% in the crust and 40% in the core.

Certain of the elements are to be found in nature in their pure state—that is, that element alone, rather than in combination with another element. Carbon is one, graphite another, as well as sulphur and the gases.

While oxygen is found alone, it is still present in countless combinations with other elements. Quartz, for example, has the formula SiO_2, meaning that quartz is made up of one atom of silicon and two atoms of oxygen. (The formula of any given mineral never varies.) Quantities of the two gases oxygen and hydrogen are present in and on the crust as water, having the formula H_2O—two atoms of hydrogen and one atom of oxygen.

A little earlier I mentioned that sometimes a crystal could form in a very short period of time. When the right combination of temperature, pressure, and saturation of a mineral is present, some trigger can and does start crystalline growth, which, once started, progresses very rapidly. In a matter of minutes, hours, or days, crystals can form, sometimes so rapidly that you can actually see them forming! An excellent example of this is the following: Make a smear of an alcoholic solution of iodine on a slide, then view it under a microscope, watching closely until the fluid begins to evaporate. Suddenly a number of tiny specks will appear in the puddle. These are the "seedling" crystals of iodine. A minute or two more for the alcohol to evaporate, and suddenly the crystals will seem to shoot up right into the lens of the microscope! They grow with amazing speed into wonderful and beautiful clusters of perfect iodine crystals. In exactly the same way clusters of larger crystals, such as quartz, grow in nature.

Now, breathe gently on the slide, immediately returning your eye to the microscope, and the moisture in your breath will melt the cluster of crystals until they slump down into a puddle again. Once more, the solution will evaporate, and once more the crystals will solidify and grow rapidly into a cluster, this time having an entirely different shape and position from the first

Kits like this are used to grow crystals and crystal clusters at home.

time. Again and again you can melt them down and watch them grow, in an absolutely fascinating display of atomic movement.

Kits are available today in department stores and rock shops for the growing of crystals of several different kinds. With these you can "manufacture" a group of crystals that are in every way the same as those found in nature. Rock candy is another example of crystalline growth. In this case, crystals of sugar are reformed by hanging a string in a supersaturated solution of sugar and allowing crystals to form in clusters attached to the string.

There are a great number of rocks which are not suitable for cutting gemstones, due either to their lack of distinguishing characteristics, color, hardness, or because of some other deficiency. The deficiency is only from the point of view of the gem cutter, however. The rock itself may make an outstanding cabinet specimen.

2.

Characteristics
of Rocks and Minerals

The geologist has various methods of identifying and classifying rocks and minerals. But before describing these, it might be well to explain just what sort of specimen interests the collector.

Micro specimens are tiny fragments mounted on a support. Because of their small size, they are viewed through a magnifying glass. The collecting and mounting of "micro-mounts," as they are called, is a special area of collecting which will be discussed at greater length in a later chapter of this book.

Next up the scale of size come the "thumbnail" mounts. These are specimens of minerals or rocks large enough to be seen easily with the naked eye—about the size of your thumbnail.

After the thumbnail comes the cabinet-specimen size, and these may range from a piece about the size of your fist, to huge chunks too heavy to lift. The range of the specimens a person may decide to collect is related to the amount of space available, the size of the cabinet shelf or drawer he keeps them in, and the availability of the mineral or rock itself, together with the cost of the specimens if they are purchased.

Needless to say, museums and institutions are the places where the largest specimens can be seen, and usually this large cabinet sample is called a museum specimen, rather than a cabinet specimen. To the avid rockhound, or perhaps I should say mineral collector—because "rockhound" does have a rather special connotation—a trip through an institution such as the Smithsonian results in mixed emotions. After looking for years for a specimen of some rare material, and finally being forced to purchase, say, a thumbnail-sized piece for more dollars than you can truly afford, it is slightly frustrating to stand before a display case and gaze at a chunk of the same material a couple of feet across.

The size specimen usually collected is the average cabinet size, about like your fist. First, these are more easily handled than the smaller sizes, and they make a very good showing in a cabinet drawer or shelf. In the case of mineral crystals, naturally enough, the effort is to obtain the largest crystal possible which is intact with all or most of the faces visible. In the case of quartz and a few other minerals, clusters of such crystals are available, and these are attractive and imposing parts of any collection.

In collecting minerals and rocks, it is very important to label each specimen accurately and to find some method of keeping that mineral and its label together. The label should include the name of the mineral or rock, where it was found, the date found, and if known, the finder. If you purchased the specimen, then you should ask the dealer or person from whom you purchased the specimen for the information concerning the location, identity, etc. Sometimes the dealer will not know anything about the pieces he sells. It is better, if you are a serious collector, to pass up such specimens and wait until you find them in another shop where the dealer knows more about his stock.

Often, too, you will find a dealer who, when asked for information, will glibly rattle off a set of statistics which you can accept as true or not, as you wish. It is a good policy to check, as far as you can, the occurrence of that material in the location given, before you label the specimen for identification.

Despite all the trouble it is to keep a good identifying system, a collection without such a system loses much, if not most, of its value. Minerals are not alone in this. Any collection of almost anything connected with the earth sciences — nature, ecology, or natural history — is of very little value unless each and every specimen is accurately identified, together with all pertinent information.

ROCK CHARACTERISTICS

Rocks are identified by several different qualities or physical properties. Among these are *hardness, color, luster, streak, specific gravity* or *weight*, and *cleavage*. Obviously, not all of these can be determined in the field while collecting. However, a few may be, and these will help considerably in the preliminary identification of the rock you are holding. Another characteristic of some rocks is fluorescence, which is the subject of a separate chapter.

Hardness

Hardness of rocks is determined by a more or less arbitrary scale developed so that anyone with materials found in any home or laboratory can classify a specimen. This is called the Moh Scale, and it is graduated in steps from 1 to 10. Each step does not necessarily mean that the one above or below it is twice as hard or half as hard. The difference between Step 9 and Step 10, for example, is very great as compared with the difference between Step 1 and Step 2.

In simple layman's language, the Moh Scale can be described thus:

Step 1: TALC. The softest mineral, capable of being scratched by every other mineral, and also easily scratched by the fingernail. Feels greasy.
Step 2: GYPSUM. Scratched by the fingernail, but not easily.
Step 3: CALCITE. Capable of being scratched by a sharp penny. Very easily cut with a steel knife blade.

Step 4: FLUORITE. Easily scratched with a knife blade.

Step 5: APATITE. Can be scratched with difficulty by a steel point, and it will itself, also with difficulty, scratch glass.

Step 6: FELDSPAR. A steel blade barely leaves a mark, but a file will scratch it easily. It will scratch glass readily.

Step 7: QUARTZ. This mineral will very easily scratch glass, copper, steel, or almost any common substance.

Step 8: TOPAZ. Topaz will scratch quartz easily, and is harder than almost any common substance.

Step 9: CORUNDUM. Easily scratches both quartz and topaz. Several man-made products are as hard as corundum, but differ chemically. Carborundum is one of these.

Step 10: DIAMOND. This is the hardest substance found in nature or in man-made materials. It easily scratches corundum. Because of its hardness, diamond is very important in industry as a cutting and grinding material.

In determining hardness in the field, quartz, feldspar, and calcite are very common almost everywhere, and every field trip should include a knife and some kind of glass in its equipment. Even an old bottle will serve admirably.

Color

Color determinations in the field are relatively easy to make — you simply look at the specimen — except in instances where the specimen may be covered with a layer of a different mineral, such as clay, indurated volcanic ash, or some other concealing addition. Oxidized layers are the most common concealing layer, and when they are present, one can reveal the color of the specimen by chipping the surface to expose the inner mineral. All the nodules of Brazilian agate imported to this country have been chipped, not to identify the material as agate, but to see if the inside is more colorful than normal. If it is more colorful, the price is raised as premium material. Unfortunately, this chipping more often than not causes the nodule to crack in one or more places, thus ruining much of the agate for cutting purposes. Nothing can be done about this condition, however, since it is the native collectors in the field who are responsible. If the specimen were destined to become a cabinet specimen, this chipping would not be so bad, since the nodule would be left in the whole, or at most, a face sliced off and the remaining surface of the nodule polished.

The color of a specimen does not necessarily indicate that it is a solid piece of one element or another. Color is most often caused by minute-to-large quantities of an accidental impurity. The importance of color in identification is the fact that many minerals are found only with some impurity or other which colors that particular mineral. Other minerals are never found with any color other than that which is characteristic of that substance. Malachite and azurite, for example, are always a deep green or blue, opaque, and are easily recognized as copper minerals.

In transparent minerals, the color may be rich and deep or so pale as to be almost undetectable. Amethyst is a good example of this variable staining during the formation of the crystals. Since one of the factors regulating the price or value of a gem material is its color, it follows that pale amethyst is far less valuable than a specimen with a deep, solid plum color.

Many minerals have their color found in zones. Others are dichroic. There is a difference in the two terms. Zoned color is found most dramatically in tourmaline of the "watermelon" variety. Here the outer layers of the crystals are a deep, bright green, while the inner core is pink to rose or deep red, resembling a slice of watermelon; hence the name.

This zoning of color is apparent no matter which way you look at the specimen, while dichroism is another matter entirely. Here again, tourmaline is a good example of this phenomenon. Viewed through the sides of the crystal, a specimen may show a bright-green color, but viewed through the ends of the same crystal, the color may be a dirty brownish-green to almost black.

Luster

Luster is another way of identifying or partly identifying a mineral. This is the appearance of the freshly exposed surface. Rocks

and minerals are divided into two rough categories as to luster—metallic and nonmetallic. Metallic luster appears like
metal, sometimes with a color overlaying the surface, usually
yellow or yellowish, since the luster is usually due to the inclusion of sulphides in the specimen.

The nonmetallic luster is further broken down into several
categories: *silky*, in the case of asbestos and other fibrous materials; *vitreous*, if the surface looks porcelaneous, such as smithsonite; *resinous*, as in the case of amber, and in some of the
wood opals; *adamantine*, if it has a hard, somewhat greasy look,
as is seen in diamond, mercury, lead, and other elements; *pearly*,
where cleavage planes show as flakes or cracks beneath the surface; *glassy*, as in garnets. All these properties are indications of
certain kinds of minerals, and all serve to help identify the specimen to a certain degree. At the very least, they place the specimen within a certain group where positive identification becomes more sure.

Streak

Related to color, and a test that is easily performed in the field, is
the *streak test*. This is nothing more than scratching the mineral
on a dull, unglazed surface, such as the back of a bathroom tile,
or on the surface of a special streak tile sold for the purpose, and
observing the color of the powder left by the streak. Often the
color of the streak is entirely different from the color of the specimen, and this makes the streak test a valuable one for identification.

The hardness of a tile is about 7, so minerals harder than
this will not leave a streak, but will scratch the tile. This in itself
is an indication of identity. For such minerals, a very small chip
pounded into a fine powder will serve much the same purpose as
the streak by showing the color of the powder. If the powder is
placed on a sheet of white paper, or upon some other white surface, the color will show up more clearly.

The streak test shows black when iron pyrites are drawn across the tile.

A scratch test being made on glass. The crystals of quartz scratch the plate easily.

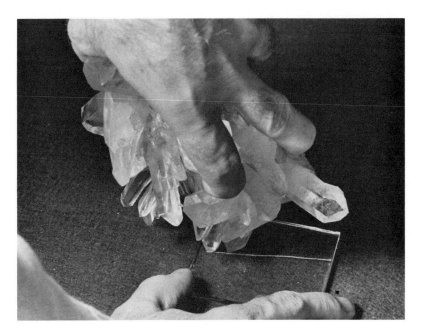

Specific Gravity

Specific gravity determinations are not easily made in the field, since one must use a specific gravity scale and make accurate measurements. In essence a specific gravity scale is one which has a double pan on the specimen end, one pan suspended below the other. In use, a beaker of water is placed under the pans, and the lower one immersed in the water until the specimen is entirely submerged. The scale is balanced with the lower pan in the water and nothing on the other pans. Now the specimen is weighed on the pan still in the air and the exact weight noted on a pad. The specimen is then removed and placed on the pan under water and weighed a second time.

The weight of the specimen under water is now subtracted from the weight of the specimen in the air. This gives you the weight of the amount of water displaced by the specimen. The weight of the specimen in the air is now divided by the weight of the displaced water. The result is the specific gravity of the specimen.

Naturally, this determination is only accurate in identifying pure minerals. If you were working with a rock composed of several different minerals, the answer would be meaningless, since it would represent the combination of the specific gravities of all the minerals.

An example of a specific-gravity determination follows: A piece of the mineral in question weighs 25 grams in the air, and 15.75 grams in the water. The difference between the two weights is 9.25 grams. This is the loss of weight in water. Now divide the weight in air by the loss of weight, and the result is 2.71. That figure, 2.71, is the specific gravity of calcite. (For purposes of illustrating the method in this book, the numbers given have all been rounded out somewhat.)

Many liquids of high density which match the specific gravity of different minerals can be used for the determination of specific gravity, but this necessitates having a particular fluid for each mineral, which could run into a very sizable shelf of fluids.

Pycnometers are specially constructed laboratory bottles used for the determination of specific gravity. However, all these methods are no more accurate for the amateur than the simple double-pan balance, and it would appear that the balance is the most practical method to use; especially since such a balance could be rigged up by anyone who is at all handy with his hands. The balance itself need be nothing more than an arm balanced in the middle with a single pan on one end and the double pan on the other. Some method of balancing the arm must be provided, usually in the form of a long, narrow screw upon which a nut can be rotated closer to or farther from the balance point until the arm is balanced at the zero point. After this, any number of weights may be used on the single pan, and these weights should be as accurate as possible. Sets of balance weights are available from school lab supply houses and some of the larger hobby shops.

Cleavage and Fracture

Cleavage and fracture are often confused by the beginner. They are really manifestations of different properties. Cleavage is the parting plane of a mineral, and it is related to the atomic structure of the crystal. This permits a crystal to part along the atomic planes in a smooth, flat surface. The direction of a cleavage plane is always identical in every crystal of the same mineral, in relation to the axis of that crystal.

Fracture, on the other hand, is the way a mineral or crystal will break if subjected to pressure or sudden impact. Fracture is usually a tentative way of placing a specimen into a certain group and is not a definite identification test. In the case of testing a piece of obsidian, however, a blow at the edge of a specimen will always result in a conchoidal fracture, leaving shell-shaped surfaces which are typical of this mineral. Several other minerals also have a conchoidal fracture, but usually not to the dramatic extent of obsidian. Most rocks and minerals merely break with a rough surface, without definite identifying characteristics.

Obsidian, broken to show the distinctive conchoidal fracture.

Location

Location is also a help in mineral identification, and after you have collected awhile and become familiar with areas, you will find that certain minerals are found or not found in certain locations. For example, it is useless to look for diamonds in the United States, except within a limited area in the Southeast. While they may be found in other locations, they are not plentiful enough to warrant your going on a collecting trip in search of them.

3.

Fluorescent Minerals

I am indebted to Raytech Industries, Inc., for the information contained in this chapter.

Fluorescence is a fascinating phenomenon and one that the beginner has some difficulty understanding. The most common definition of fluorescence is "the property of emitting visible light during radiation by ultraviolet light." Most fluorescent minerals fluoresce under shortwave ultraviolet light—that is, light having a wavelength of 2537 angstroms.

This light will cause irritation and even graver consequences if shined for any length of time into the eyes. It can burn the retina of the eye, and for this reason a person should not look directly into a source of shortwave ultraviolet light.

The word *fluorescence* is taken from the name of the mineral fluorite. In the early 1800s, Sir George Stokes, the British physicist, observed a visible blue glow emitting from a specimen of fluorite. This emission was caused by the action of ultraviolet rays in direct sunlight. The scientist called this emission fluorescence, and thus it is known today.

Most of the fluorescent minerals are almost completely nondescript in ordinary lighting. They are drab and uninteresting. Yet, when placed in a darkened room, under the rays of shortwave or longwave ultraviolet light, they appear breathtakingly beautiful. The colors are vibrant, intense, and dramatic, and, I might add from sorrowful experience, very difficult to capture on color film.

Different minerals fluoresce in different colors, and these colors are always constant for that particular mineral. In fact, fluorescence is a most accurate method of identifying certain minerals.

In order to understand fluorescence, it is first necessary to understand something about the physical structure of matter. Everything on earth is made up of small particles called molecules, which in turn are made up of atoms. The atoms consist of a nucleus and electrons. The nucleus remains in the center, and the electrons revolve around the nucleus, much as do the planets around our sun.

The electrons remain in orbit just as do the planets in the solar system. The orbits in which the electrons travel are of different diameters, and each electron requires a precise amount of energy to maintain its position in its orbit. Some atoms have only one, or a few, electron orbits around their nucleus. Others have many, and some a great many orbits and, of course, a great many electrons.

If an electron had less energy, it would fall into an orbit closer to the nucleus, and if a greater amount of energy were applied to the electron, it would take a position in an orbit farther away from the nucleus. These orbits are located in what are called *electron shells,* and all orbits of a given diameter are contained in an electron shell having the same diameter.

Radiation is a form of energy, and ultraviolet light is no exception. Many minerals are sensitive to the radiation of ultraviolet light, and these minerals fluoresce and phosphoresce under that energy. When ultraviolet light is shined upon a piece of one of these minerals, the light passes through some of the atoms. When some of the energy strikes an electron, the additional energy the electron absorbs from the light causes it to move to an orbit farther away from the nucleus, to a higher energy level within the atom. The movement of this electron into the larger orbit creates a void in the electron shell it vacated. This gap must be filled in order for the atom to maintain its electrical balance.

The electrons closer to the nucleus do not have enough energy to travel out into a higher energy level, so an electron from a larger orbit must travel down into the vacant gap.

In doing so, the electron must give off some energy to match the lower energy level to which it is pulled, and this energy takes the form of visible light. It is this light which we see as fluorescence in the mineral. This tiny amount of energy given up by each electron is called a *quantum,* and when the quanta are radiated as light, they are called *photons.* In a mineral subjected to the rays of ultraviolet light, countless numbers of electrons shift to a greater orbit, absorbing the energy of the light, and an equal number of electrons shift to a lesser energy level in a smaller orbit, giving off their quanta as fluorescence. This exchange happens so rapidly that to all intents and purposes the light we see is continuous, and not flickering.

When the ultraviolet light is removed from the substance, all the electrons snap back to their normal positions in their normal orbits, and the visible light, or photons, ceases to be given off.

In some minerals, however, the electrons are slow to return to their normal orbits. Some take a second or two, others longer periods of time. Some take several hours, and some are known to take several years to return to normal. As long as the electrons are in the process of returning to their normal orbits, the mineral will continue to produce light. It is this afterglow, when the ultraviolet light is removed, that is called *phosphorescence.*

In order for a mineral to fluoresce, it must contain some impurities as an activator. Without these impurities the material will not fluoresce at all. The amount of impurity required to cause a mineral to become fluorescent is very small, and very critical — as critical, almost, as the amounts of energy required to hold the electrons in place in their orbits. The amount and the type of these impurities determine the intensity and the color of the fluorescence in that mineral.

Fluorescence has found many uses in industry and also in police work. One important use it has been put to is the tagging of postage stamps, to permit the rapid automatic sorting of mail. Airmail stamps are printed with an invisible ink which fluoresces one color, and the regular-mail stamps with an ink which fluoresces another color. The mail, all mixed up, is run through a high-speed sorting machine which has photosensitive eyes to detect the color brought into the visible spectrum by the application of ultraviolet light. Those letters bearing stamps fluorescing in one color are kicked into one bin while the others are passed on to a second bin. Many thousands of man-hours each day are saved in the sorting of millions of pieces of mail.

Another most important application of fluorescence is in the location of various minerals, such as sheelite, a valuable tungsten ore. Tungsten is one of the metals vital to our economy, and deposits of it are detected with the aid of battery-operated ultraviolet lights used at night. Night prospecting with this apparatus has yielded much valuable material.

Some minerals fluoresce better under longwave ultraviolet light — 3000 to 4000 angstroms in length — than under the shortwave ultraviolet light — 2537 angstroms. Following is a list of minerals which fluoresce, together with a table stating whether they require short- or longwave light, and whether they also phosphoresce. In Franklin, New Jersey, is a mine from which a great number of very distinctive minerals are taken. It is probably the largest source in this country.

Not all of the minerals listed here are of interest to the collector, but many of them are, and these will be found listed in the next chapter too.

There are certain abbreviations used in this list for words such as *phosphorescent, fluorescent,* etc., which are repeated often:

ph = phosphorescent, phosphorescence, phosphoresce
fl = fluorescent, fluorescence, fluoresce
lw = longwave ultraviolet light, 3000–4000 angstroms
sw = shortwave ultraviolet light, 2537 angstroms

adamite: Green under sw, paler under lw.
amber: Fl blue-white under lw.
anglesite: Yellow under sw.
aragonite: Green fl produced by sw.

axinite: Fl deep red under sw and faintly under lw. A long-lived ph is also present.

barite: White or cream color under lw.

barylite: blue-white fl under sw.

benitoite: Fl bright blue under sw.

brucite: Fl bright blue-white under sw.

calcite: Fl almost every color of the rainbow. From Texas comes a species that fl and ph blue under sw and pink under lw.

calcium larsenite: A rare mineral found only at Franklin, New Jersey. Fl brilliant chartreuse under sw and dull yellow under lw.

calomel: Fl brick red under sw.

celestite: Blue under both sw and lw; has a greenish-white ph.

cerussite: Yellow fl under lw.

chondrodite: A bright golden yellow, and yellow-orange to buff under sw.

clinohedrite: Fl a golden brown under sw, with ph also present.

colemanite: White or cream under both sw and lw, and also some ph.

corundum: Deep red under lw.

curtisite: Sw produces white, cream, and pale green swirls and patterns in this mineral.

deweylite: White under both lw and sw.

diamond: Fl green, orange, red, and blue under lw.

dumortierite: Blue-white fl under sw.

eucryptite: Cerise under sw. A most unusual and beautiful color.

fluorite: Fl brilliant blue under lw. Paler under sw.

hackmanite: Brilliant apricot under lw, pale apricot under sw.

hyalite: Brilliant green under sw.

hydrozincite: Blue-white under sw.

manganapatite: Buff-brown to bright golden yellow under sw.

margarosanite: A brilliant blue-white fl under sw.

norbergite: Fl bright-yellow to dull buff under sw.

opal: green under sw, lesser intensity under lw.

pectolite: Bright-yellow to cream under sw, gold ph under sw.

petalite: Fl white under lw and sw.

phlogopite: Buff-yellow under sw.

phosgenite: Yellow under sw.

powellite: Cream or golden under sw.

scapolite (wernerite): Brilliant yellow under lw. This is one of the most spectacular fl minerals activated by lw. Also ph weakly.

sheelite: Bright blue under sw.

sodalite: Golden-brown under lw.

sphalerite: Orange or golden-brown under lw.

spinel: Brilliant red under lw.

stolzite: Fl greenish-white under both lw and sw.

svabite: Fl a bright golden-brown under sw.

talc: Fl creamy white or pale greenish-white under sw.

terlinguaite: Bright yellow under sw.

tremolite: Orange under both sw and lw.

willemite: Very brilliant green under sw.

witherite: Fl bright blue-white under both lw and sw.

wollastonite: Brilliant orange fl under sw. This rare mineral is found at Franklin, New Jersey.

zircon: Golden-yellow to brown under sw.

4.

Rocks and
Minerals for the Collector

To aid the beginner in recognizing some of the more common minerals and rocks, I am listing about 100 species with their most apparent features. Please bear in mind, however, that many rocks and minerals occur in a variety of colors and forms, so if you do come across a specimen which does not fit any of the descriptions, do not be discouraged – you merely have to look a little further for the identification. Also bear in mind that not all of the rocks described here are to be found in the United States. Some of them are found in other countries, but since there is no regulation that says a person cannot be a rockhound anywhere in the world, these rocks have been included in the list. The great majority of them are found in our own country, though, and most of them are to be found in quantity. Some are rare.

actinolite   A metamorphic mineral, either white, light green, dark green, or violet. When violet, it is called *hexagonite*. It has a glassy luster, a hardness of from 5 to 6, specific gravity of 3.0 to 3.3, and has an uneven fracture. The mineral has a prismatic cleavage and is translucent to transparent. Some of the material is fluorescent. Actinolite is found in a great many locations throughout the United States (see **tremolite**)

adularia   One of the Orthoclase minerals mostly found in Switzerland. Forms vary from colorless to white prismatic crystals, sometimes quite large. Adularia has a glassy luster, a hardness of 6, and a specific gravity of 2.6. The fracture is conchoidal, and the material cleaves on two 90-degree planes.

almandine   This beautiful mineral is one of the garnet group. It occurs in igneous rocks as crystals, varying in size from specks to as large as a walnut or larger. It is found all over the world, but in New York State is so plentiful that it is mined and the mineral crushed for use as the coating on garnet paper, an abrasive used in woodworking. The color is deep violet-red, and the hardness is 6.5 to 7.5. The specific gravity is 4.3, which makes almandine one of the heaviest of the garnets. The fracture is conchoidal, and there is no cleavage plane. The mineral is translucent to transparent. See also **andradite, grossularite, pyrope, spessartite,** and **uvarovite.**

amazonite, amazonstone   See **microline.**

amblygonite   This scarce mineral is found in several locations throughout the world, the best quality coming from Burma, Brazil and Maine. It is found in pegmatites as crystals, some of them large, and is colorless to white, light gray-green, gray-blue, and lilac. It has a glassy luster, a hardness of 5.5 to 6.0, and a specific gravity of 3.0 to 3.1. It cleaves easily, and the fracture is uneven. Used for faceting gemstones.

analcime (analcite)   Small, clear to colorless, greenish or reddish crystals occurring in trap rock associated with zeolites. Found in New Jersey, Michigan, Colorado, and in Nova Scotia and other countries. Hardness is 5.0 to 5.5 and specific gravity 2.3. The fracture is subconchoidal, and the material cleaves well. It is translucent to transparent, and the crystals are usually so small that it is difficult to obtain gemstones of any size from them.

anatase Blue, yellow, and brown crystals, occurring as well-defined pyramidal crystals in seams and veins associated with, or on, quartz. It is found in Colorado, Massachusetts, and North Carolina, as well as in Brazil and several other countries. The hardness is 5.5 to 6.0 and the specific gravity 3.8 to 3.9. Perfect cleavage and subconchoidal fracture. The mineral is translucent to transparent. The transparent crystals have a high refractive index, and in earlier times the mineral was mistaken for diamond by many geologists and gemologists. See also **brookite, rutile.**

andalusite Found in metamorphic rocks associated with granite intrusions. Clear crystals displaying dichroism when cut into faceted stones, green across the axis and red parallel to the axis. The gem variety comes from Brazil and Ceylon. The luster is glassy and the hardness 7.5 with a conchoidal fracture. Specific gravity is 3.1 to 3.2. Fair cleavage. See also **chiastolite.**

andadrite This is another of the garnet group, and is found in seams of igneous and metamorphic rock. Colored from yellow-green to emerald green and from tan to brown and black, the hardness is 6.5 to 7.5, specific gravity 3.8. Transparent with a conchoidal fracture. The green type is called **demantoid,** and is one of the loveliest gemstones known. See also **almandine, grossularite, pyrope, spessartite,** and **uvarovite.**

anhydrite Gem crystals of this material are quite rare and are found in very small sizes. The color is clear, white, gray, and lilac. It is a soft material, 3.0 to 3.5 in hardness, with a specific gravity of 3.0. The fracture is uneven, and the mineral cleaves in three planes. It is sometimes fluorescent. Found in New York and New Jersey and in Switzerland, Germany, Poland, and other countries.

apophylite Found in many areas of the United States, and in many foreign countries, among which are India, Iceland, Germany, Mexico, and Nova Scotia. Colorless to white, pink, and green with a pearly luster, a hardness of from 4.5 to 5.0 and a specific gravity of 2.3 to 2.4. Fractures unevenly and cleaves in one plane.

aragonite While this mineral is a little soft for use as a gem material, still some beautiful stones have been cut from it, and in a collection of unset gems it finds an important niche. Colorless to white or pale yellow, aragonite has a vitreous luster, hardness of 3.5 to 4.0 and a specific gravity of 2.9. The fracture is sub-conchoidal, and it does not cleave. It is found in England, Spain, Mexico, and other countries, as well as in the United States. This is more of a specimen mineral than a gemstone.

augelite This little known mineral forms colorless crystals up to about an inch in all directions. With a hardness of 4.5 to 5.0 it can be faceted into gems resembling quartz. Luster is glassy and the specific gravity is 2.7. The fracture is conchoidal, and the mineral has two cleavage planes. Augelite is translucent to transparent, and is sometimes found in rose or yellowish crystals. Found in several locations in the United States and in several foreign countries.

axinite Crystals of axinite can be as large as two inches or more, and the best material comes from France, although recently discovered deposits in California have yielded excellent crystals. Brown, gray, yellow and greenish-yellow are the commonest colors, and the crystals are translucent to transparent, with a hardness of 7.0 and a specific gravity of 3.3. The fracture is conchoidal and the material has a cleavage plane.

azurite This is one of the most beautiful of the copper minerals, but because of its softness, gemstones cut from it must be set in some manner so as to protect the surface from wear and contact. The color is light blue to nearly black, hardness 3.5, luster glassy, and specific gravity 3.8. The fracture is conchoidal. Azurite is always found in association with malachite.

barite The mineral is colorless, bluish, reddish, brown, and in-between shades. It is found in sedimentary rock and in veins. "Desert Roses," a type of barite which crystallizes in petal-like forms in sand, are found in several locations in this country, and in foreign countries as well. The hardness is 3.5, specific gravity 4.6, luster glassy, and the fracture is uneven. Barite is one of the minerals found inside septarian nodules.

benitoite So far, the only source of this material is in a dike in a serpentine deposit in San Benito County, California, from which location the mineral takes its name. Crystals are blue and white, hardness is 6.5, and they have a specific gravity of 3.6. The fracture is conchoidal, the luster glassy, and the mineral is translucent to transparent. It fluoresces blue.

beryl This gem mineral is found in pegmatite deposits, and sometimes forms as crystals several feet long! It occurs as translucent-to-transparent crystals, either blue, white, pink, green, or yellow. Its hardness is 8, making it a good mineral for gemstones, the specific gravity is 2.6 to 2.8, and the luster is glassy. The fracture is conchoidal. Beryl is the mineralogical name of some of the most valuable and important gemstones. Emerald is its green form; morganite is pink or purplish; aquamarine is pale blue or various tints, including blue-green; golden beryl is yellow; and goshenite is colorless.

beryllonite A rare mineral found only on a very few locations in this country, such as Stoneham and Newry in Maine. The occurrence is decomposed pegmatite veins. Beryllonite has a hardness of 5.5 to 6.0, a specific gravity of 2.8, and a conchoidal fracture. The crystals are translucent to transparent, and are remarkably well formed, from an inch or more across.

calcite Comes in so many different types that it would be impossible to list and describe them all in a volume of this limited scope. Indeed, an entire book could be devoted to the different kinds of calcite. One of the most common minerals on earth, with varieties that make wonderful specimens for the cabinet or drawer, but do not lend themselves well to the cutting and polishing of gemstones, mostly because the hardness is only 3.0. The specific gravity is 2.7. Still, many lapidaries have cut calcite, and when successfully done, the mineral makes attractive faceted stones for a collection of unset material. About the only way they could be worn in jewelry is as earrings or as a pendant where the stone would not be subjected to physical wear. Much calcite is fluorescent, and some of the colors, mainly a deep orange-red or reddish orange, are very pronounced under the short-wave ultraviolet light. Clusters of magnificent crystals, often covered with a druse of small-to-tiny crystals of another mineral, are common from the mines of Mexico.

cassiterite   One of the tin minerals, cassiterite is found as transparent material, and as dark, reddish-brown nodules. The transparent mineral is used for faceting, and the dark material for cutting cabochons. Hardness is 7.0 and the specific gravity is 7.1 — very heavy. The fracture is uneven. Bolivia produces the finest material, but there are good deposits in New England, Virginia, and other places. Cassiterite is one of the most important economic sources of tin.

celestite   Blue, white, or reddish-brown, with a hardness of 3.5 and a specific gravity of 4.0. The fracture is uneven, and the luster is glassy. Sometimes the crystals are striped blue and white. Found in many countries, but the best quality is here in the United States, especially around Lake Erie and in Ohio, Kansas, Colorado, and Pennsylvania.

cerussite   An important ore of lead. Crystals colorless to yellow and gray, hardness 3.5, specific gravity 6.6, fracture conchoidal, and the luster is adamantine. Good for specimen gems or as cabinet specimens. Excellent material is found in the Mammoth Mine, at Tiger, Arizona, but the best material comes from Tsumeb, Southwest Africa.

chrysocolla Pure chrysocolla is so soft that it is difficult to use as a gem material. However, chrysocolla-impregnated quartz is hard enough for the purpose and is a very beautiful material. Sky blue to green, hardness (pure) 2.0, specific gravity 2.4, with a dull, earthy luster and a conchoidal fracture. When in quartz, the hardness is 7.0 or higher, and the material often has hollows lined with tiny quartz crystal terminations. Arizona and New Mexico are the best collecting locations in this country. Good material is also found in Africa, South America, and in some European countries.

colemanite The crystals of this borax mineral are sometimes cut as curiosities, but the mineral is so fragile that gems faceted from it cannot be worn without danger of fracturing. Clear colorless or white, the hardness is 4.0 to 4.5, specific gravity is 2.4 and the fracture is subconchoidal. Luster is glassy. Found in the lake beds of southern California.

cordierite This mineral is found in Connecticut and in the Northwest Territories, Canada, but the best specimens come from Finland, Norway, Ceylon, and other countries. Dichroic, the crystals are purplish-blue to grayish-blue in one direction, and yellow to clear in the other. Hardness 7.0 to 7.5, specific gravity 2.6, glassy luster with subconchoidal fracture. Translucent to transparent, the latter usually being used for faceting and the former for cabochon cutting of gemstones. See also **dichroite** and **iolite.**

corundum In common with beryl, corundum has many gem varieties, ruby and sapphire being the best known. Transparent to translucent, specific gravity 3.9 to 4.1, fracture uneven, and luster adamantine. This mineral is the hardest known except for diamond—9.0 on the Moh Scale. Ceylon, Africa, and South America are the most important sources of corundum minerals, although some may be found in Montana and in North Carolina. Corundum, as emery, is mined in New York and other states for use as an abrasive.

cristobalite This mineral is quartz with impurities, and has a hardness of 7.0, with a glassy luster and a specific gravity of 2.3. It occurs in such small crystals that it is unsuitable for cutting, but it does make a good cabinet specimen. It is found in California, Colorado, and Mexico.

danburite Found in several countries, notably Switzerland, Japan — where the finest crystals are obtained — and the United States. It was first discovered near Danbury, Connecticut, for which location the mineral was named. Hardness is 7.0, specific gravity 3.0, glassy luster, and colorless to white, gray, brownish, and yellow. Good specimens are remarkably clear and sparkling when cut.

datolite Occurs in both crystalline and massive form. The crystals are light yellow-green, hardness 5.0, specific gravity 2.8 to 3.0, with a glassy luster. Translucent to transparent. Datolite is associated with zeolites in cavities in trap rock. Nevada, California, Michigan, and New Jersey are some of the localities in this country where the mineral is to be found, as well as in several foreign countries.

diamond This mineral hardly needs description, and it is found only in one location in this country — Arkansas. There have been a very few diamonds discovered in other localities, but never in sufficient quantity to warrant a collecting site. Most of the diamonds of the world are taken from South Africa. The hardest material known, 10 on the Moh Scale, with a specific gravity of 3.5, adamantine luster, conchoidal fracture, and colorless to black. The great bulk of diamonds are used as industrial tools, only a small portion of them being suitable for gemstones.

dichroite One of the names given to the mineral cordierite because of the property of dichroism — the phenomenon of showing a different color from a different angle of view. See **cordierite.**

diopside Crystals white, light to dark green and brown, with a hardness of 6.0, specific gravity of 3.5, glassy luster, and a conchoidal fracture. The best crystals in this country come from St. Lawrence County, New York. Other locations are California, Quebec, Italy, and Austria. Transparent to translucent, small faceted gems are cut from this beautiful material.

dioptase Emerald-green, glassy luster, and a specific gravity of 3.4, hardness 5.0. This is a greatly sought-after mineral for rock collectors. Not much good dioptase is to be found in our country, the finest specimens coming from Tsumeb, Southwest Africa. Good crystals have been taken from the Mammoth Mine in Tiger, Arizona, as drusy crusts associated with willemite and wulfenite. There is a magnificent geode lined with spectacular dioptase crystals at the Smithsonian Institute in Washington, D.C.

dolomite Valuable as cabinet specimens of a very interesting mineral, crystals occur as a layer on other rock. Pinkish, white, or pastel tints. Dolomite has a hardness of 3.5, specific gravity of 2.8, and a pearly luster. Translucent to transparent. The fracture is conchoidal.

dumortierite Another mineral that is better suited as a cabinet specimen than as a gem material, the violet-to-pink-and-blue crystals have a hardness of 7.0, specific gravity of 3.4 and a glassy or pearly luster. Common in the Western states, this mineral is mined and used as a ceramic dielectric in automobile sparkplugs.

enstatite Clear crystals of this mineral are cut into faceted gems. These come from India, and from the Kimberly diamond mines in South Africa. Gray, green, or yellow, a hardness of 5.5 to 6.0, specific gravity 3.9, luster silky, fracture uneven, translucent to transparent. Enstatite is a magnesium silicate. When iron is present, the mineral is called *hypersthene*.

epidote   Dichroic crystals show green from one direction and brown from another. The hardness is 6.5, specific gravity 3.4 fracture uneven, and luster glassy. Translucent to transparent, pistachio green to light yellow-brown. Found in Alaska, North Carolina, California, and in Europe, in metamorphic rocks, pegmatites, traprocks in association with zeolites, and in limestones. Transparent crystals are cut into faceted gemstones, and the opaque material makes fine cabochons.

fluorite   Colorless, white, black, brown, violet, yellow, and blue, fluorite forms masses of cubes intergrowing through one another, making an impressive cabinet specimen. The green variety is sometimes cut into faceted gemstones, but it is very soft and should be worn only with precaution against abrasion and wear. Hardness 4.0, specific gravity 3.0, luster glassy, and fracture conchoidal. The mineral often fluoresces. Found in cavities in sedimentary rocks. Some very spectacular crystal groupings have been taken. Fluorite is abundant in the United States and in several European countries.

grossularite   This mineral is one of the garnet group, and comes as pink crystals or massive green material. California, Oregon, Mexico, and Africa are the main locations where this material may be found. Hardness 7.0, specific gravity 3.5, conchoidal fracture, and glassy luster. See also **almandine, andradite, pyrope, spessartite,** and **uvarovite.**

gypsum   An important commercial mineral, mined for the manufacture of plaster of paris. It is found as massive deposits in sedimentary rocks and as free crystals in limestone voids. Colorless to white with silky luster, hardness 2.0, specific gravity 2.3. Some gypsum is fluorescent. One form of this mineral is selenite. The mineral is useful and interesting as cabinet specimens, but it is entirely too soft to be cut into gemstones. It is found nearly everywhere in the United States and also in Europe.

hematite   The most important ore of iron, hematite is called *bloodstone* and *Alaska diamond*. This is not the true bloodstone, which is another mineral entirely, but hematite is so called because of the way it "bleeds" bright red when it is worked. The red stains everything and is very difficult to remove. The hardness varies from that of talc up to 6.0 or even higher. The luster is metallic and the specific gravity is about 5.0. Uneven fracture. Hematite is usually cut as a flat-based stone, faceted on the top, and takes a polish so brilliant that it appears as a black mirror. It is usually cut in Germany. Not many lapidaries like to cut this material because of the mess it makes with the red stain over everything in the shop.

hiddenite   See **spodumene.**

howlite   "Cauliflower stone," this mineral is a soft calcium silicoborate found in the borax deposits of California and other locations. It is pure white, but there may be gray streaks throughout each nodule, at which time interesting cabochons may be cut from it. Hardness 3.5, specific gravity 2.6, luster sub-vitreous, and fracture even.

hypersthene   Hypersthene and enstatite are identical minerals, except that the former has iron in the chemical composition, making it a magnesium iron silicate instead of a plain magnesium silicate. All physical properties apply. See **enstatite.**

idocrase   Also known by the names *vesuvianite, californite,* and *cyprine.* Hardness 6.5, specific gravity 3.5, luster glassy, fracture uneven. As californite it is cut into cabochon gemstones. Rarely is idocrase found in crystals transparent enough and solid enough to cut into small faceted stones. Found in limestone deposits associated with garnet and other minerals. Vermont, New Jersey, New York, Arkansas, and California are some of the locations where this mineral may be found.

ilmenite   This mineral is much the same as hematite, except for the addition of titanium. It is black to brownish-red, hardness is 6.0, specific gravity is 4.7, and the fracture is conchoidal. Sometimes cabochons are cut from ilmenite, which is found in metamorphic rocks and in pegmatites in New York, California, Quebec, and several foreign countries.

iolite   See **cordierite.**

jadeite   This mineral and nephrite (which see) are both commonly called "jade". It occurs in many locations in California, Mexico, Burma, Japan, and elsewhere. Colors range from white to emerald green, yellow-green, brown, violet, lilac, and reddish brown. Hardness from 6.5 to 7.0 and specific gravity 3.3 to 3.5. The fracture is splintery, and the material is very difficult to break, being an exceptionally tough mineral, which is one reason for its value and popularity as a carving medium, especially high in the esteem of Chinese craftsmen. The translucent varieties are more valuable than the opaque kinds, and the translucent emerald green most valuable of all.

kunzite   Gem crystals of the mineral spodumene are called kunzite when their color is lilac. Fairly rare and quite valuable. Named after Dr. George F. Kunz, an eminent authority on gems and gem materials. See **spodumene.**

kyanite   Green, blue, to colorless, hardness 5.0 to 7.0 in different directions on the crystal, specific gravity 3.6 to 3.8, fracture splintery, translucent to transparent. Kyanite is found in many places in the eastern United States and is especially abundant in New England, Virginia, North Carolina, and Georgia.

lazulite   Bright-blue material found in pegmatites and metamorphic rocks in California, Georgia, and New Hampshire, as well as in South America and other localities. Hardness 5.5 and specific gravity 3.4, with an uneven fracture. The mineral is translucent to transparent and is used for cutting cabochons.

lazurite Found in metamorphosed limestones, usually in masses of blue to violet-blue material with a glassy luster, hardness of 5.5 and specific gravity of 2.5. The fracture is uneven, and the mineral is translucent. Lazurite makes beautiful cabochons. See **sodalite.**

lepidolite A mica mineral found in masses in pegmatites and commonly used for carving, ash trays, pen stands, etc. Hardness 2.5 to 4.0, specific gravity 3.0, translucent to transparent. Takes a good polish and, because of its softness, can be worked with steel tools. Maine and California are the two principal sources of this material.

leucite Gray to white and colorless, sometimes transparent crystals of small size are located in recent lava flows. Hardness 5.5 to 6.0. Specific gravity is 2.4, and the fracture is conchoidal. The best source is Italy, but good crystals are to be found in Magnet Cove, Arkansas; Leucite Hills, Wyoming; and in several other locations in North America.

magnesite Found in sedimentary beds in association with serpentine and also as transparent, colorless crystals. Hardness 3.5 to 5.0, specific gravity 3.0, smooth fracture. The crystals are cut into faceted gemstones. Found in Staten Island, New York, and in Washington and California, as well as other localities, including Brazil.

malachite Arizona is the best location in this country for malachite, and some spectacular specimens have been taken from Bisbee at the Copper Queen Mine. Hardness is 3.5 to 4.0. Specific gravity 3.9 to 4.0. Opaque to translucent, splintery fracture. The mineral is a deep, rich green, varying from light to dark and blue-green. It is highly prized among gem cutters and jewelers, despite the softness, and gemstones cut from the material have a good value. The stones should not be subjected to hard wear. The best material now comes from Katanga, Africa, since our own supplies are nearly exhausted. Malachite is associated with azurite, and sometimes forms as a velvety coating of minute vertical crystals on masses of azurite.

marcasite An iron sulphide which in earlier years was much in vogue when cut as small stones, faceted on top and flat on the bottom, used as encrusting stones on jewelry. Sometimes hundreds of these tiny gems would be set into a single ornament. It is still used today, but not nearly to the same extent. Hardness 6.0 to 6.5, specific gravity 4.9, metallic luster, uneven fracture, opaque brassy-yellow masses found in sedimentary rocks in many locations throughout the world, and in this country in Missouri and Wisconsin. See also **pyrite.**

mesolite Very similar to natrolite. Mesolite is found in white, pale pink, and yellow masses, and cuts into beautiful cabochons with a chatoyant surface. Hardness 5.0, specific gravity 2.2. Comes from Oregon, New Jersey, and sites in Canada.

microcline While this mineral may be found in white, flesh, and reddish-brown colors, the green variety is the one prized for stone cutting. When green, microcline is called *amazonite* or *amazonstone*. Opaque, sometimes translucent, hardness 6.0, specific gravity 2.5 to 2.6 with a conchoidal fracture. Found in pegmatites at Pikes Peak, Colorado, the best comes from Amelia, Virginia, and from Ontario and Quebec in Canada.

microlite Found in pegmatite dikes in New England and New Mexico, and the yellow-brown and green-brown crystals are found in mines at Amelia, Virginia. Yellow crystals are also common. Hardness 5.5, specific gravity 4.2 to 6.4. Resinous luster, translucent to transparent. The crystals from the Virginia mines make good faceting material.

mimetite This mineral is rather rare in the United States, but it does occur in Utah near Eureka. Mexico, Tsumeb in South Africa, and Saxony are the best locations for the variety known as *campylite*. This form is in botryoidal masses, ranging from white through yellow and yellow-brown to brown. Hardness is 3.5 and specific gravity 7.0 to 7.3. The fracture is uneven, and the crystals are translucent to transparent. Cabochons are sometimes cut from mimetite.

moonstone One of the orthoclase feldspars. Moonstone is colorless to whitish, translucent to transparent, with a beautiful play of blue color as the stone is moved. Cut as cabochons. Found in New Mexico, but the best quality comes from Ceylon and Madagascar. See **orthoclase.**

natrolite Found in zeolite associations as colorless-to-white crystals having a hardness of 5.0 to 5.5 and a specific gravity of 2.2. The fracture is uneven, and the luster is glassy. Used for faceted gemstones, the best material in this country comes from Livingston, Montana, and Summit, New Jersey. Switzerland, Italy, and Bohemia are other locations, and there are deposits in many more countries.

nepheline Occurs in igneous rocks as colorless, white, gray, or reddish crystals with a hardness of 5.5 to 6.0, specific gravity 2.5 to 2.6, subconchoidal fracture, and translucent to transparent. Most of this mineral is found in Russia and in Ontario, Canada.

nephrite Along the Fraser River Valley in British Columbia are tremendous deposits of nephrite of excellent quality. Good material is also to be gathered in California, Wyoming, and Alaska. The best comes from Wyoming. Hardness 6.0 to 6.5, specific gravity 2.9 to 3.02, and fracture uneven. Comes in several colors, but the green and the white are the most sought after. Tough and difficult to work, this material is often made into such items as ornamental steak knives, which hold their edges practically indefinitely. Cabochons, beads, and carvings are other uses of nephrite. See also **jadeite.**

obsidian An amorphous volcanic glass which has been cooled so rapidly that it had no time to form crystals. Found in the

United States in entire cliffs, one such being the famous Obsidian Cliff in the Yellowstone National Park (where collecting is illegal). Its hardness is 5.0, specific gravity 2.3, luster glassy, fracture conchoidal. Obsidian is abundant in several varieties, from dense opaque black to translucent black. That variety having streaks of brown through it is called *mahogany obsidian*. A variety containing white inclusions is known as *snowflake obsidian*. The material takes a wonderful polish, is easy to work, and makes beautiful cabochon gemstones. Glass Buttes, Oregon, and Montgomery Pass in California are two localities where obsidian is abundant, and there are many other prolific collecting sites throughout the West. *Apache tears* are small nodules of obsidian. An excellent material for the novice lapidary.

olivine Olivine is a common rock-forming mineral, and is common also in meteorites. It is really a series of minerals known under several names, such as chrysolite, peridot, fayalite, and dunite. As dunite it occurs in huge masses. As peridot it is found as transparent crystals of a deep yellow-green. Hardness is 6.5 to 7.0. The specific gravity is 3.3 to 3.4, and the fracture is conchoidal. Peridot is the gem variety. Olivine is so abundant in certain locations that there is a beach in Hawaii made of olivine sand! The green sand is beautiful against the blue water of the tropical Pacific. Arizona and New Mexico are the two best areas in this country. Found also in Burma and in several European countries, as well as in Hawaii.

opal While there are several kinds of opal, much of it common material without any play of color, we are mainly interested in this volume in discussing precious opals of the varieties prized for gemstones. To most people, when opal is mentioned, Australia immediately comes to mind as the source of this beautiful mineral. Many do not know that the most beautiful and the most valuable opal in the entire world is found in Virgin Valley, Nevada. Opal is also found in many other locations in this country but none of it has the fire, color, and quality of the Virgin Valley material. Hardness 5.0 to 6.0, specific gravity 1.9 to 2.2, resinous luster, fracture conchoidal. There are several varieties. White opal is translucent to opaque, showing flakes of color throughout. Black opal is black or gray with play of color. Black opal is the most strikingly beautiful variety. Fire opal is transparent reddish-orange with flakes of color deep inside. Jelly opal is perfectly clear and transparent with soft colors playing inside, but not in well-defined flakes as in black or white opal. See Chapter 9 on working opal and other difficult gem materials.

orthoclase　Found in igneous rocks and metamorphic rocks, orthoclase is of interest as gem material in certain varieties as noted above. As a mineral specimen it has a hardness of 6, glassy luster, specific gravity of 2.6, and conchoidal fracture. Excellent crystals can be found at Robinson, Colorado, and at Good Springs, Nevada. See also **adularia, moonstone, sanidine.**

pectolite　Found in association with zeolites in traprock cavities. Hardness 5.0, specific gravity 2.7, splintery fracture, and silky luster. Pectolite is very fibrous and is easily separated, and the fibers will irritate your skin by penetrating much like fiberglass. Makes cabochons with a beautiful silky luster. Can be found in Paterson, New Jersey; Magnet Cove, Arkansas; Isle Royale, Michigan; and in other localities. White to gray and reddish.

peridot　See **olivine.**

phenakite　A mineral found in pegmatites in free crystals, usually fractured. Colorless to white, hardness 7.5 to 8.0, specific gravity 3.0, conchoidal fracture, and glassy luster. Obtained in several locations in Colorado. Mt. Antero, Pikes Peak, and Colorado Springs are some of the best places. Also found in Maine, Wyoming, Brazil, and some European countries.

plagioclase　This is the name covering a group of minerals ranging from sodium aluminum silicates to calcium aluminum silicates. The colors run from white through yellow to reddish-gray and black. Hardness is 6.0 and specific gravity varies from

2.6 to 2.8. Luster is glassy and fracture conchoidal. Perhaps the most striking of the varieties is *labradorite,* a gray mineral having an intense iridescent sheen in two directions, called *Schiller flash.* This color may vary in different specimens from metallic yellow through blue to metallic green, with mixtures of all three at times. Labradorite may be found in New York, Utah, California, and Labrador, as well as in several other localities.

pyrite   Identical with marcasite, except that marcasite has a fraction more sulphur in its composition. Pyrite is usually a little lighter than marcasite, and is often known as "fools gold," since it can be mistaken for gold by amateur prospectors. See **marcasite.**

pyrope   Pyrope is the deep yellow-red garnet found in igneous rocks in Arizona, New Mexico, and South Africa. The specific gravity is 3.5, and the hardness is 7.5. During the early part of this century pyrope was used extensively in small-faceted stones to make rather garish jewelry solidly encrusted with the gems. Bohemia was the center of this industry. See also **almandine, andradite, grossularite, spessartite, uvarovite.**

quartz   More than half of the earth's crust is composed of quartz in one form or another. It is the most common mineral we know, and it is the basic constituent of innumerable other minerals. Agate, opal, chalcedony, jasper, and carnelian, to name a few out of literally hundreds of materials, all are quartz. Many books have been written about this single mineral. As a matter of fact, quartz is so prevalent that we have come to think only of its transparent or translucent form as "quartz," and to call its other forms by other names. It is because of this practice that a great many people are unaware that the lovely gemstone they are wearing is merely another manifestation of this ubiquitous substance. Pure quartz is colorless to white, with a hardness of 7.0 and a specific gravity of 2.6, a conchoidal fracture, and a glassy luster. It is found almost everywhere in the world. Spectacular crystal clusters are found in Hot Springs, Arkansas, and, as

"Herkimer diamonds," at Little Falls, New York. Excellent *smoky quartz* comes from the Pikes Peak, Colorado, area, as does *rose quartz*, which also is found in Maine.

rhodochrosite Found in veins as massive material, this manganese mineral is strikingly colored in bands of different shades of pink. Extremely heavy and soft, it is difficult to work because of the zones of varying hardness, from 3.5 to 4.0. Specific gravity is 3.4 to 3.6 and the fracture is conchoidal. Translucent to transparent, and also opaque. Found in Montana and Colorado, the latter having the best specimens. Also found in great quantities in Argentina and Brazil. Mexico, Germany, and other countries also yield this mineral, which, for all its abundance, still commands a high price as cutting rough.

rhodonite Although this is an entirely different mineral, it is often confused by beginners with rhodochrosite, above, probably because of the similarity of the names. Rhodonite is found in much the same situations as rhodochrosite, and is also a manganese mineral. It is granular in appearance, and when cut and polished as a cabochon, the surface shows as a myriad of small flakes, each one throwing a brilliance. Rhodonite is often streaked with gray or black. Hardness is 5.5 to 6.0, specific gravity 3.7, fracture splintery, and luster glassy. The best material comes from Franklin, New Jersey, the source of many wonderful fluorescent mineral specimens. It is also found in Massachusetts and in many countries in Europe.

rhyolite This is not a pure mineral, but rather a metamorphic rock containing masses of quartz in several different shapes. Impregnated with copper, rhyolite is an interesting material which cuts into beautiful cabochon gemstones. As such it is more often known as *copper rhyolite*, rather than just rhyolite. Green to pink with reddish hues and brown in streaks or patches. Found in Adams County, Pennsylvania, where it is known as *cuprite*. Also found in Utah, Montana, Colorado, and many other areas. As cuprite the hardness is 3.5 to 4.0, specific gravity is 5.8 to 6.1, the fracture is conchoidal, and the mineral is translucent.

rutile   This mineral is only rarely found in crystals large enough to cut into gemstones. Usual habit is to form needles and needle-like masses, and often these are grown inside clear quartz crystals, making a most interesting mineral called, obviously enough, *rutilated quartz*. While the needle type is black in appearance, the crystals also form in reddish to golden color. When crystals of the reddish color are found, they are suitable for making faceted gems. Rutile is also made synthetically. Hardness is 6.0 to 6.5, the specific gravity 4.3, fracture uneven, and luster adamantine to metallic. Found in pegmatites, gneiss, and schists in Hiddenite, North Carolina, and in Georgia, Arkansas, Vermont, and many other locations and countries. Infinitesimal needle inclusions in other minerals are responsible for the occurrence of the "stars" in asteriated quartz, star rubies, etc.

sanidine   Sanidine is an orthoclase feldspar with a blue adularescence, and is known better by the name *moonstone*. See **moonstone** and **orthoclase.**

scheelite   Found in veins of quartz and metamorphic deposits, this little-known mineral occurs as white, light-green and light-brown crystals, translucent to transparent. Found in Kern County, California, in Mojave and Cochise counties, Arizona, and in Utah, Connecticut, and foreign countries. Hardness 5.0, specific gravity 5.9, luster adamantine, and fracture uneven.

selenite   See **gypsum.**

serpentine   This material occurs as grainy masses of enormous proportions. It is so plentiful and easy to mine that it is often used as a building stone. It is colored white, green, yellow, brown, red, and black, and in any combination of these colors in stripes and stains. Some serpentine is translucent and useful for carved ornaments, ashtrays, bookends, and similar objects.

Hardness varies from 2.0 to 5.0 and the specific gravity from 2.2 to 2.6. The fracture is uneven, luster waxy, and some of it is fluorescent. Found in great masses at Brewster, New York; Hoboken, New Jersey; Staten Island, New York; and in Vermont, California, and in many other localities in this country and elsewhere. Serpentine is known under many different names, such as *verde antique, williamsite, bowenite, marmolite,* and *chrysotile.*

shattuckite   A compact fibrous copper mineral, beautiful but rare. It is found in the copper mines of Arizona. Hardness is 3.5 and specific gravity is 3.8. It is deep blue and green, usually mixed with impurities which cause considerable difficulty when polishing a gemstone of this material. However, if care is taken in working shattuckite, the resulting jewel is well worth the time and trouble.

sillimanite   Found in mica schists and in metamorphic deposits. Rather rare. The mineral is for the most part fibrous and massive, but clear crystals do occur and are prized as gem material. The crystals are clear light blue, hardness 7.5, specific gravity 3.3, fracture splintery, and luster glassy. Found in Massachusetts, New York, Pennsylvania, and Connecticut, as well as Ceylon and Brazil, where the gem varieties originate.

smithsonite   Rarely found in crystals large enough or good enough to use for faceted gemstones, smithsonite is usually cut as cabochons. A zinc ore, this mineral is found as crusts, both botryoidal and mammillary, sometimes very thick. White, yellow, bluish and greenish, the hardness is 5.0, specific gravity 4.3 to 4.4, conchoidal fracture, translucent, with a vitreous luster. Found in Magdalena, New Mexico; Leadville, Colorado; Arkansas; Tsumeb, Southwest Africa; and in several foreign countries.

sodalite   A mineral having an intense blue color, rather rare in pure form as cutting material. It is also known in colorless,

white, and violet shades. When the material is pink it is called
hackmanite. Hardness 5.5 to 6.0, specific gravity 2.3, glassy luster, and conchoidal fracture. About the only location for collecting sodalite in this country is at Litchfield, Maine. The finest
deep rich blue sodalite and excellent hackmanite comes from the
Princess Quarry at Bancroft, Ontario, Canada. The Ice River area
of British Columbia also yields good sodalite. Cut into cabochons, the mineral makes striking gemstones. Often streaked
with matrix rock in shades of gray.

spessartite Spessartite is one of the garnet group. It can be dark
brown, reddish and pinkish, or orange, and sometimes black.
Found in rhyolites and metamorphic rocks. Hardness 6.5 to 7.5,
specific gravity 4.2. The luster is glassy, and the fracture conchoidal. The best material comes from Amelia, Virginia;
Nathrop, Colorado; the Thomas Range in Utah; Ramona, California; and from South America and other countries. See also **almandine, andradite, grossularite, pyrope,** and **uvarovite.**

sphalerite An interesting mineral, this zinc sulphide comes as
crystals in yellow, red, orange, brown, green, and, rarely, colorless. Hardness is 3.5 to 4.0 and the specific gravity 3.9 to 4.1.
Fracture conchoidal, luster resinous. Sphalerite is sometimes
fluorescent, and when so, is also triboluminescent. If lightly
stroked with another stone or a knife blade, this mineral will
emit flashes of orange light. In Utah; Franklin, New Jersey; Missouri; Tiffin, Ohio; and in several foreign countries.

sphene See **titanite.**

spinel Found in igneous and metamorphic rocks, and in pegmatites. Occurs in almost any color, and is also synthesized.
Hardness 7.5 to 8.0, specific gravity 3.5 to 4.1, and the fracture is
conchoidal with a glassy luster. Found in Amity, New York;
Helena, Montana; New Jersey; and in Ceylon, Burma, and Thai-
land.

spodumene   This is a lithium aluminum silicate, which, when occurring in different colors, is known under different names. Found in pegmatites, almost exclusively. The lilac variety is called *kunzite,* and this is a highly prized gem material. Bluish-green spodumene is known as *hiddenite.* Hardness 6.5 to 7.0, specific gravity 3.1 to 3.2, fracture uneven, and luster glassy. The two colors mentioned are transparent. Hiddenite is found at Hiddenite, North Carolina, whence the mineral takes its name. Kunzite occurs in the Pala, California, area, and spodumene is also found in New Mexico and South Dakota; Newry, Maine; and in Brazil and other countries.

staurolite   Known as "Fairy Crosses," staurolite is found generally as twinned crystals growing through each other to make a cross. Recently, because of their popularity, counterfeits are being made of brown clay for sale through rock shops and gem dealers. If you collect your own, you are more sure of the genuine mineral. Dark brown, opaque to rarely transparent, hardness 7.0 to 7.5, specific gravity 3.6 to 3.7, fracture subconchoidal, and luster glassy. Found in Fairfax County, Virginia, and in Georgia, New Mexico, and other locations.

titanite   Occurs in metamorphic and igneous rocks, as brown, yellow, green, and gray crystals, transparent and sometimes very thin. Hardness is 5.0 to 5.5 and specific gravity 3.4 to 3.5. Conchoidal fracture and adamantine luster. Found at Bridgewater, Pennsylvania; Brewster, New York; Renfrew, Ontario; some of the Western states; and in Canada and Mexico. See also **sphene.**

topaz   One of the most popular gem materials and commanding good prices, topaz occurs in many colors, the most highly prized being blue, shades of brown, and colorless. Found in pegmatites and in cavities in rhyolite rocks. Hardness 8.0, specific gravity 3.5 to 3.6, conchoidal fracture, and glassy luster. Colorado, Texas, California, Maine, Virginia, and Utah are some of the locations in the United States where topaz may be found. Brazil is also an excellent source of this mineral. Many inferior minerals are sold as topaz, usually with some qualifying name preceding, such as "golden topaz" or "Spanish topaz."

tourmaline Occurring in many colors and clear, and in combinations of two colors, tourmaline has been given different names by gem dealers to differentiate the varied colors. Thus, the red variety is called *rubellite*, the green mineral *tourmaline*, and the blue variety *indicolite*. Found in igneous and metamorphic rocks, and the best crystals in pegmatites. Hardness 7.0 to 7.5, specific gravity 3.0 to 3.3, fracture uneven, and luster glassy. Tourmaline is found almost everywhere. The New England states, New York, California, Brazil, Madagascar, and Russia are some of the locations.

tremolite See **actinolite.**

turquoise An opaque copper mineral in shades of blue and sometimes green. The more green in turquoise, the less value it has. The most highly prized material is an intense light blue. It is found in veins in rocks of desert regions. Hardness is 5.0 to 6.0, specific gravity 2.8, porcelaneous luster, and smooth fracture. New Mexico, Nevada, Arizona, and Colorado are the best states for finding this highly prized mineral, as well as South America.

ulexite As a gem mineral, ulexite is almost completely impractical because of its softness, but more so because, on exposure to air, the surface decomposes into a white coating or rind, concealing the silky appearance of the mineral. As a cabinet specimen ulexite is of interest just because of these properties. Found in desert borax deposits, hardness 1.0, specific gravity 1.6, white, translucent, with a silky luster and a cottony fracture. Found in the Mojave Desert in Nevada and in California and South America. As an experiment I cut and polished a cabochon of ulexite to produce a gemstone with an amazingly beautiful chatoyant surface. The gem held its beauty for perhaps four or five months, slowly losing the luster and finally becoming entirely chalky white with no shine or luster remaining.

utahlite See **variscite.**

uvarovite This is a green garnet of great beauty, but it does not occur in the United States to my knowledge, except for minimal deposits in Maryland, Arizona, California, and New Mexico. Uvarovite is associated with chromium ores. Specific gravity 3.8, hardness and fracture the same as the other minerals in this group. See also **almandine, andradite, pyrope, grossularite, spessartite.**

variscite An aluminum phosphate mineral closely resembling turquoise, but colored yellow-green, and commonly penetrated with veins of dark brown or gray. This mineral used to be known as *utahlite*, because of its discovery in Utah. It occurs in veins and nodules. Hardness 3.5 to 4.5, specific gravity 2.2 to 2.8, porcelaneous luster, and smooth fracture. Found in Utah, Arkansas, and some foreign countries.

willemite Usually white or colorless, this mineral is also pale blue. From deposits in the Western part of the country. It is strongly fluorescent and shows a characteristic brilliant, metallic green under the short-wave light. Hardness 5.5, specific gravity 3.9, with an uneven fracture and a glassy luster. Willemite is best known to the collector from the Franklin, New Jersey, deposits of zinc, where it is found as small inclusions in rock. This material makes interesting cabochons and beautiful spheres, especially when they are viewed under the short-wave light. Also found in the Mammoth Mine at Tiger, Arizona, and in Belgium.

wulfenite Occurring in plates or tubular crystals in unmistakable clusters. The color and the shape will serve to identify immediately this beautiful mineral. Yellow, orange, or brown, hardness 2.7 to 3.0, and specific gravity 6.8. The fracture is subconchoidal and the luster adamantine. Translucent to transparent. The Red Cloud Mine in Yuma County, Arizona, produces most spectacular crystals, and wulfenite is found all over the Southwestern states, as well as in Mexico and Europe. A highly prized cabinet mineral, and useful in cutting rare faceted gem-stones.

zircon   Found in granite rocks and pegmatites, and as loose pebbles in sands and gravels in stream beds. Brownish and reddish, zircon turns a brilliant blue or colorless upon heating. The high refractive index permits a wonderful color flash, and colorless zircons were for a long time (until the advent of the modern synthetics such as Yag) used as substitute diamonds. Hardness is 6.5 to 7.5, specific gravity 4.0 to 4.7, fracture conchoidal, luster adamantine. Zircon is found in North Carolina, New Jersey, New York, Pennsylvania, and in some Western states, as well as Canada and other countries. Valued as gem-cutting material for faceted stones.

zoisite   Found in metamorphic and igneous rocks, and in pegmatites in gray, brown, or pink crystals. When pink, the mineral is known as *thulite*. Hardness is 6.0 and specific gravity 3.4. Glassy luster, uneven fracture, translucent, sometimes fluorescent. Found in Mitchell County, North Carolina, and throughout New England in pegmatites and metamorphic rocks. California, Tennessee, and foreign countries also list deposits.

5.

Collecting Sites

Knowing where to look for minerals is as important as knowing what to look for, and knowing what you have after you have found it. There are a great number of collecting-site publications available, and a list of them will appear later in this book for your convenience.

One very helpful occupation is a visit to as many museums as are within convenient traveling distance, to view the collections of minerals and rocks on display. Familiarization with these display specimens will be of inestimable help when you go on a collecting trip of your own. Visiting every rock shop in your vicinity is also a very valuable way to familiarize yourself with the appearance of minerals in the raw, so to speak.

Pick up and handle the rough specimens offered in these shops. Look at them closely, so you will be able to recognize another piece of the same material when next you see it. Pay attention particularly to the outer surface and whether it is the same as the inside. In other words, is the outer surface different from the mineral itself? Often a specific mineral will appear completely different when it is lying on the ground, or when it is freshly dug up. Jade is a classic example of this, and there are many true stories about hunters for jade kicking lumps of it out of their way, while they spend days, or even weeks, looking for the valuable green stone without success. Jade oxidizes, and the

pieces become covered with an opaque white rind, entirely concealing the color within. On one very rich collecting site in the
Northwest, the ground was literally covered with troublesome
white rocks, tripping collectors and turning their ankles, but not
one single fragment of jade was visible. Needless to say, there
were many red faces when the word got around that the white
rocks were oxidized jade boulders.

Amethyst is another mineral which is often concealed by a
rind—of hematite, of calcite, or of some other mineral having a
different aspect from that of amethyst. The difference is, however, that the crystals so concealed are still in the shape of
crystals, and thus could be of value even if they were of material
other than amethyst.

For the serious mineral collector any trip should be well
planned in advance and a definite purpose decided upon. Just
going outdoors and idly picking up rocks with the hope of find-

The abrasive action of water and sand has exposed veins of minerals
along this mountain stream in Idaho.

ing a good or valuable specimen is a complete waste of time and energy. Going to areas known by local names is nearly as useless. The names given to places do not necessarily mean that those places are rich collecting sites. I do not know how many "agate beaches" there are in the United States, but to go to one with the idea that most of the pebbles on that beach are agates is sheer folly. Such a place could very well have come by its name simply because, in the days before the area was settled, someone found an agate there. In telling about his find, he could refer to the place as "the agate beach," and as such the locality could become known. True, where one agate was found, it is reasonable to assume there are others, but they may be so sparse that you would spend weeks looking fruitlessly for gem material.

Many rock shops, especially those in the Western part of the country, have lists of collecting sites, either for their state or for their immediate vicinity. The owners usually are also willing to tell you where to go to look for good specimens.

Chambers of Commerce of most cities will be able to supply you with lists of mineral locations, and government bulletins are available listing the locations of important minerals in the country.

Mining companies are sometimes an excellent source for collecting, especially in the tailing dumps. However, permission *must* be obtained from the mine superintendent before trying to look for material. Also, safety precautions must be observed when working over such locations. A hard hat, gloves, heavy shoes (preferably of the safety kind, which will protect your feet from being crushed if a heavy rock falls on them), and goggles should be part of your standard collecting equipment. They should be *worn*, not permitted to lie unused in the trunk of your car. A 4- or 5-pound sledge, a couple of chisels, and a gad point, together with a good, strong prybar and a mineral scoop, are about all the items needed for collecting. A strong shovel is also very useful, especially in mine dumps.

Road cuts are sometimes very rich in newly exposed mineral deposits, especially new road cuts. If you are fortunate enough to live near a place where a road is being put through, and they are

Mine dumps where trucks haul the tailings are often excellent sources of minerals. Get permission from the mine company before entering any dump.

Cuts like this, severing a large rock formation, are good places to look for minerals.

An inclusion of calcite or quartz along a road cut. Look for these as a possible source of collectible minerals.

blasting cuts through land and rock rises, you should take every advantage of the loosened rock to glean for minerals. Remember that you simply cannot go there to run all over the place while crews are working. Remember also that working a freshly blasted area can be very dangerous, since rock slides are common, and if you are caught in one you may be seriously injured. The slide does not necessarily have to be a natural one—you yourself can cause a slide by prying out a rock that was acting as a keystone and releasing many tons of loose rubble.

It is good practice and common sense not to work under a ledge in such places and not to pry out a large boulder before making absolutely sure that it is not a keystone. If you are in the *least* doubt—leave it alone. It is also plain common sense never to go collecting alone, but to go with someone who, if not more experienced than yourself, can at least assist in the digging and

A septarian nodule from Utah as it comes from the ground, looking like a ball of mud or clay.

removal of rubble. Too, a partner can always go for help if needed, and this may save lives in time of emergency.

You must remember that rockhounding is hard work at times, and sometimes requires strenuous digging and lifting of heavy stones. Much dirt and rubble must be shoveled out of the way to search for the elusive minerals, but when finally discovered, they offer a thrill of accomplishment no other endeavor quite equals.

It is a good idea to become a member of the nearest rock club. If it is an established club, some of the members are sure to have been on collecting trips, or vacation trips, and can tell you where they found minerals and gemstones. Rarely indeed will you find a true rockhound to be secretive about the location of his finds.

If no club is near your vicinity, then it is an easy matter to start one. Your place of business, your church, the local merchants, all will be found willing to post a neat bulletin advertising the fact that a rock club is in the making. After enough interested persons make themselves known, you can begin to organize the club. A letter to the secretary of an already established club or to one of the national or federated clubs will bring all the information you need to get started.

A subscription to one of the leading rock and mineral magazines will provide you with a good source of information. Usually these magazines list new collecting sites as they are discovered and reported, information on other sources of material, addresses of rock shops, and companies dealing in supplies and tools pertinent to the hobby.

Many persons owning large tracts of land in different states lease out collecting rights to interested people, either by the hour, day, or week. The Priday Ranch, in the Northwest, where one can collect thunder eggs, and the famous Woodward Ranch in Texas, where agates may be collected, are a couple of examples. These places charge a fee for collecting by the day, and sometimes charge per pound for everything you find. Some also maintain a shop where material collected from their lands is for sale to those who do not wish to go through the labor of

The rock ledge at the Herkimer field. It is regularly blasted and bull-dozed so collectors can search out the elusive crystals in pockets of the matrix rock.

searching themselves. In the Southeast are diamond and emerald collecting sites run on the same basis. The owners periodically bulldoze the overfill away to expose new rock, and a few very valuable stones have been discovered by lucky persons. This kind of collecting appears unrewarding to me, however, since the actual stones found are so few and far between that it is almost a waste of time to try for any. Yet, the fact remains that every once in a while a veritable tyro at the game will walk in, pay the fee, and become the discoverer of a gemstone that makes him wealthy.

There are many fee-collecting sites scattered all over the country, the bulk of them being west of the Mississippi River. The majority of rock shops are also in the western half of the country, mainly because collecting is so much better in the Midwest to Far West, especially in the Northwestern states. These states are very aware of the tourist attraction they have in their surface minerals, and take some time and trouble to work up site maps and information on collecting trips and fee sites. These are given free of charge by the Chambers of Commerce and by the individual rock shops.

A list of such collecting sites is appended here, together with any pertinent information available at the time of this writing. The sites are arranged alphabetically by states, and the addresses given are actual mailing addresses to which you may write for additional information if you desire.

While I have been in correspondence with every site listed here, you must bear in mind the possibility of a site's no longer being in existence by the time you want to go there. Many factors change conditions in a collecting site. Natural causes such as slides, earthquakes, and floods, or just plain over-collecting, will eliminate an area. Perhaps the owner sells his place and the new

This outcropping was ground smooth and round by the action of a glacier. If veins of different minerals are exposed there is a good chance of finding pockets of good cutting or specimen materials.

Throwing water on the collecting site helps greatly by washing away the chips and dust, and by emphasizing the contrast between the gem material and the base rock.

The Western mountain streams are another good place to look for agates and more precious gem pebbles, such as sapphires.

owner does not care to continue having the public work on his land. Or a highway may have been cut through an area, ruining it for collecting. An owner may die and the land revert to heirs or even to the state, thus closing it to fee collectors.

For these reasons it is always a good idea, when planning a collecting trip, to write to the places you would like to visit and plan your itinerary according to the response you receive from them. Most of the site owners will respond very rapidly to your inquiries, especially if you enclose a stamped, addressed envelope with your letter.

There are roughly 1,500 rock shops, large and small, in the United States-far too many to list here. They are all listed, along with rock clubs, product manufacturers, etc., every year in the April issue of *The Lapidary Journal,* which is on sale all year in rock shops and the larger general magazine stores. It costs only $1.75.

Pockets like these in the surface of the ground often contain collectible minerals.

Alaska

Atlanta House, Mile 166 Glenn Highway, Palmer, Alaska 99643. Fossils are to be found at this collecting site where you may spend a day for the fee of $1 per person. The fee includes the loan of a rock pick, and a guide to the digging area. Camping is available at the site, which is open June 1 through August 15. Closed on Monday.

Arizona

Dobell Curio, Donald J. Patton, P.O.Box 914, Holbrook, Arizona 86025. Located 19 miles east of Holbrook on Highway 180 East, at the south entrance to the Petrified Forest National Monument, this rock shop operates collecting sites for petrified wood at the rate of 30¢ per pound for all material up to 100 pounds. Over 100 pounds, the rate drops to 20¢ per pound. Clubs going as a group are given the lower rate regardless of the quantity gathered. Petrified wood is also sold at the shop, as well as Mexican geodes. Open seven days a week all year. Mr. Patton cautions collectors that his water is bad, and that you should bring your own drinking and cooking water if you intend to camp there for any length of time. No charge for camping space.

Royal Purple Mines, R. & S. Jewelcraft, P.O.Box 543, Loop 10 East, Quartzite, Arizona 85346. Located 5 miles off Highway 395, between Davis Creek and Pine Creek, California, this mine yields rainbow obsidian. The owners live in Arizona, but you should write to the following address for information and a map to the mine: Royal Purple Mines, New Pine Creek, Oregon 97635, Attention: Mr. and Mrs. Ray Griffith. The fee of $3 per person entitles you to collect 20 pounds of material. All over that amount is charged for at the rate of 15¢ per pound. Extensive camping grounds with good spring water open May 1 to October 15.

Apache Tears Cave and Rock Shop, Box 7, Superior, Arizona 85273. Operates a collecting site for a fee of 50¢ per person where you may look for fluorescent geodes, rhyolites and Apache Tears. You may collect approximately 10 pounds for the fee. Buckets and tools are supplied by the shop. Camping area is available at the site, which is open all year. The location is about 3 miles south of Superior on State Highway 177. Signs mark the way.

Arkansas

Mount Ida Mines, Ocus Stanley, P.O.Box 163, Mount Ida, Arkansas 71957. The owner has two mine sites where quartz crystals may be dug. He has no set fee, but "You pay what you want to," according to Mr. Stanley. Camping at and near the sites, and he has a shop at his home address. The mines are never closed. Collectors either phone Mr. Stanley in Mount Ida or go to his home, where detailed instructions as to how to reach his mines are available.

Crater of Diamonds, Route 2, Murfreesboro, Arkansas 71958, is the only place in the United States where one can go to hunt for gem diamonds. Several very large stones have been taken from this site over the past few years. The fee is $2 per person per day. Screens and tools are supplied at the office. Located 2½ miles south of Murfreesboro on State Highway 301. Signs lead the way. Camping at Lake Greeson, 6 miles north, and there are motels and restaurants in Murfreesboro. There is a rock shop at the site.

Coleman's Crystal Yard, Jessieville, Arkansas 71949. This is a site where quartz crystals and clusters may be gathered for a fee of $2 per person, which entitles them to collect all the quartz they find. Prybars to loosen the crystals are furnished free by the Colemans. They also sell minerals at their shop. Camping sites about 6 miles away. Their place is open seven days a week all year. To get to Jessieville, drive north from Hot Springs on Route 7 for 15 miles.

California

Snyder ranch, Betty Snyder, Valley Springs, California 95252. This site is located about 2 miles east of Valley Springs on County Road 12. The fee is about $4.00 per day ($1.50 for children 12–15 years old, $0.75 for children 6–11 years old) which entitles the collector to pick up 100 pounds of material. Moss agate, opal, jasper, serpentine, and California jade are reported to be found at this site, as well as nickel ores. Camping areas at the site, and three more 3 miles from site. The ranch is open every day all year. Valley Springs is located about 55 miles southeast of Sacramento.

Imperial Valley Development Agency, Imperial, California 92251. This company provides a map of the Imperial Valley collecting sites on receipt of a stamped self-addressed envelope. There are so many areas for collecting in this fabulous valley that I simply urge you to get a map from the company, and wish you good hunting. There are nearly 100 different minerals to be found in the different locations. Here, indeed, is a place which is excellent for planning a several-week vacation collecting trip.

Calico Silver Lace Onyx Mine., Harold H. Holman, P.O. Box 686, Yermo, California 92398. The owner maintains a rock shop where he sells minerals and cutting materials. His mine is open to fee collecting, about $4.00 per person, with a 20-pound limit. The mine contains scenic onyx, and transportation is supplied to and from the mine site. Camping is available at the nearby town of Calico, as well as on the desert area at the mine. Mr. Holman requires the signing of an injury release before a collector is permitted into the mine. The rock shop is open from around 8:00 until 6:00 seven days a week, and the tour to the mine is by reservation.

Colorado

Kelly's Rock Shop, Mack, Colorado. Located at Exit 2 of Interstate Highway 70, on Highway 6-50, 12 miles east of the Utah state line. The fee of $40 per day includes a guide and a 4-wheel-drive vehicle. The site is open all year, depending on the weather, and petrified dinosaur bone is the main mineral found. The shop sells other minerals and gem material. Camping areas are available near the site.

Georgia

The Rock Shop, Box 62, Ball Ground, Georgia 30107. Oscar Robertson operates the Cherokee Staurolite Trail, where one may find the lovely "Fairy Crosses" of staurolite, tourmaline, and some gold. I have been unable to obtain information on the fee for this site, but the location is 50 miles north of Atlanta on Highway 5, and it is open from March to October.

Blackburn State Park, Dawsonville, Georgia 30534. The Resident Superintendent is located at the park, 7 miles southwest of Dahlonega on State Highway 9E, near Auraria. The mailing address is Route 3 (Auraria) Dawsonville, Georgia 30635. At the park you may pan for gold for the fee of $1 per person per day. Camping is available at the park, which covers 239 acres. Some other minerals are also available at the collecting grounds, which are open from May to October. Closed on Monday.

Crisson Mine and Gold Hills Mine, Dahlonega, Georgia, the county seat of Lumpkin County. Here is also located a gold museum. Early in the 1800s a branch of the U.S. Mint was located in this town, to mint gold coins from the metal mined in the area. Now collectors and rockhounds may pan for gold at the two above sites for the daily fee of $1.50 for adults and $1 for children. While pans are supplied, it might be better to have your own pan and shovel. The site is open weekends in April and May, and daily from June through the "leaf season." I should judge this to be around October. Campsites are available.

Idaho

Spencer Opal Mines, P.O. Box 113, Spencer, Idaho 83446. You may also write to the office in Idaho Falls for information, brochures, and a map. The address is: Spencer Opal Mines, 1862 Rainier Street, Idaho Falls, Idaho 83401. You apply at the Spencer office for your permit to dig, and from there a bus takes you to the site. The bus leaves Spencer at 8:00 a.m. and 10:00 a.m. sharp, and returns at 4:00 p.m. The bus is free. The fee is $15 per person, and the mineral found is precious opal. The fee entitles you to collect up to 5 pounds of material. All other material is charged for at a cost of $2 per pound. There is a guarantee of sorts, in that if you feel you have not received your money's worth, you leave all you have collected and your fee is returned to you. You are requested to bring your own hammers, picks, and a sledge if you have one. Safety glasses and a hard hat and safety shoes should be worn as a matter of course. You will need a bucket for washing your material.

Maine

Perham's Maine Mineral Store Inc., Trap Corner, Junction Routes 26 and 219, West Paris, Maine 04289. This store is the source of collecting information concerning five quarries in the immediate vicinity. The quarries charge a fee of $1 for each person, and the store provides information as to where, how, and when to collect. There are camping sites and motels in the vicinity. The store is open daily from 9:00 to 5:00, Sundays from 1:00 to 5:00 p.m. Closed Thanksgiving and Christmas. Smoky quartz and rose quartz may be collected, and several fluorescent minerals.

Mt. Mica Mine, Paris, Maine. Operated by Mrs. Sarah Irish Spencer, 756 Somerset Street, Rumford, Maine 04276. She also sells minerals at the Rumford address. The collecting fee is $1 per person over 12 years of age, and the pegmatite minerals such as tourmaline are to be found at her site. There is parking at the site, but the nearest campsite is about 19 miles away. The mine is open every day all year round. Contact Mrs. Spencer for appointment and details.

Minnesota

Thompsonite Beach, Mr. and Mrs. Maurice S. Feigal, Milepost 103½, Lutsen, Minnesota 55612. On the shores of Gitchie Gumie, the Feigals have built a lovely motel and gem shop, right near the volcanic flow containing the wonderful mineral thompsonite. The Feigals do not charge a fee, but will guide you to collecting areas, and each evening they demonstrate their methods of extracting the precious gem material from the basalt rock in which it is found. This service is extended only to their

Collecting minerals with a sledge hammer and chisel is hard work. Here thompsonites are being mined on the shore of Lake Superior.

motel customers. Jewelry making is also demonstrated, and the cutting and polishing of thompsonites, lintonite and other zeolites found in the area. For any rockhound making a trip through the north-central portion of the country, a stopover at the Thompsonite Beach Motel is almost a must. No one need go home without thompsonites. Camping areas are also available near the site for anyone wishing to go on his own. The motel is open all year.

New Hampshire

The Old Prospector, E. Foley, R. D. No. 2, Woodsville, New Hampshire 03785. Located on State Road 112, between Woodsville and North Woodstock, closer to the latter town. Mr. Foley used to act as guide, taking people on gold-panning trips in the local streams, but according to him, his customers "raised such hell" that he has discontinued guiding, and now he gathers gold-bearing gravel in buckets, and sells them to prospectors who can then pan the gravels for the yellow metal. He claims he never let a person leave without some gold. His fee is $1.50 per person. Plenty of camping areas nearby. A feature story was run on this colorful old prospector in the April 1969 issue of *Yankee Magazine*. He is open for business from April until "freeze-up time."

New Mexico

Graphic Mine, William Dobson, Magdalena, New Mexico 87825. The fee here is 75¢ per person, which entitles you to collect up to 10 pounds of material, with all excess charged for at the rate of 10¢ per pound. Iron pyrites, azurite, malachite, and other minerals are available, and there are camping spaces at the site without services. Mr. Dobson sells good-quality minerals and cutting material. The sites are open all year except for certain times when the Dobsons are attending the larger mineral shows, and during the hunting season. It would be a good idea to write him before going to his area. The mines are closed Sunday mornings. To reach the mines, take Highway 60 to Magdalena. On the east end of town look for Bill's Gem and Mineral Shop on the highway. In the window of the shop is a map giving exact location of the mine. You may phone for further information or to make reservations before driving to Magdalena, if you wish.

New York

Herkimer Diamond Grounds, Route 28, Box 434, Middleville, New York 13406. Seven miles north of Herkimer. Herkimer diamonds are not the gem diamonds so prized by jewelers. They are

A lucky find at the Herkimer Diamond collecting site.

sparkling quartz crystals, usually completely formed, most of
them doubly terminated, and they form a very acceptable addition to any mineral collection, especially as specimens still in
the matrix rock.

The fee is $2 for adults, $1 for children under 14, and the fee
entitles you to collect all day. There are camping facilities on the
site as well as toilets, wash rooms, and picnic tables. They are
open seven days a week from April 1 to November 30.

North Carolina

Franklin, Macon County. There are 23 mines in this county open
to the public on a fee-collecting basis, where the prospector may
obtain about 30 different minerals, mostly rubies, sapphires, star
garnets, and rhodolite garnets. Camping facilities abound, and
the area is readily accessible on major roads. Further information
may be obtained by writing to the Franklin Area Chamber Of
Commerce, Franklin, North Carolina 28734. Here are some of
Franklin's mines:

Arnold Ruby Mine	Mason Mountain Mine
Bradley's Ruby Mine	Mason's Sapphire Mine
Caler Ruby Mine	Mincey Mine: bronze
Cherokee Mine	Rockhound Haven Mine
Corundum Hill	Sheffield Mine
Gibson's Ruby Mine	Shuler's Ruby Mine
Gregory Ruby Mine	Yukon Mine
Holbrook's Ruby Mine	4 K's Mine
Jacob's Ruby Mine	McCook Mine

The average fee for the above mines is $3, and $2 for children
under 12. The fee covers anything the prospector finds. The
mines are open from April through October, seven days a week.
Rock shops and restaurants are at the mine sites, and camping
and motels are all over the area.

Emerald Valley Mines (American Gems Inc.), Route 1, Box 229,
Hiddenite, North Carolina 28636. Located on Route 90, about 40

miles north of Charlotte, the mines are operated 365 days a year from 8:00 a.m. until dark. The fee of $4 per day for adults, and $2 for children under 12, entitles the collector to dig for emerald, hiddenite, quartz, amethyst, aquamarine, rutile, tourmaline, and other gem minerals. Overnight camping is available at a charge of $2 per night per family. There are a picnic area, spring water, and bathrooms and outhouses at the area. The shop on the site sells materials for cutting and specimen material. The Emerald Inn is a motel located 4 miles from the mine at Taylorsville, N.C. One may telephone the inn for reservations.

Ohio

Mason's House of Flint, Box 107, Gratiot, Ohio 43740. Located about 7 miles south of Newark; turn east on County Road 312. Here interesting flints may be collected for the fee of 5¢ per pound for everything you find. There is a shop where you may purchase material if you do not care to dig for it. Information on the digging sites is available at the shop. They are open from mid-March to mid-November, every day of the week. A trailer campsite is at the digging for a charge of $2.50 per night with an electrical hookup. You will need a pick, hammer, and shovel for digging, which are not supplied by the proprietor. A letter will bring you a map card of the location.

Nether's Farm, Hopewell, Ohio 43746. A flint-hunting location. The fee is $1.25 per person, and this entitles you to collect up to 20 pounds of material. Excess is charged for at the rate of 25¢ per pound. Toilet facilities are available at the digging site, and there are five camp grounds in the immediate area. Open all year every day. A letter to John Nethers at the above address will bring a map and additional information.

Neibarger Farm, located just north of Hopewell, Ohio, You may address the Neibargers c/o Neibarger Farm, Route 1, Hopewell, Ohio 43746, and you may collect at their farm for fee of $1.25 per day per person. Flints, quartz crystals, agate and jasper are to be found there, and the fee entitles you to all you can find. Picnic tables and outdoor toilets are at the site, which is open all year seven days a week, weather permitting.

Oklahoma

Reynolds Rose Ranch, Route 4, Norman, Oklahoma 73069. The site for collecting barite roses is situated 5 miles east of Norman on Old Highway 9. No information as to fees or dates is available at the time of writing.

Oregon

Indian Creek Ranch, Roy Forman, Antelope, Oregon 97001. Located 5 miles west of Antelope on Route 218. Agatized and petrified wood are collected here at the fee of 20¢ per pound. Digging tools are required. A campsite is available, but with no services. Nearest food and lodging at Antelope, 5 miles east of diggings. They do sell petrified wood at the site, which is open from March through October, seven days a week.

Kennedy Ranch Agates, Gateway Route, Madras, Oregon 97741. Johnny Richardson's Agate Beds are located on Highway 97, 11 miles north of Madras. Open all year, weather permitting. According to directions, you drive 11 miles north from Madras on Highway 97 until you come to milepost 81. There you turn right for 3 miles to the ranch entrance. The fee is 20¢ per pound for anything you dig. Digging help is supplied if desired. You should bring your own digging tools. Thunder eggs, agates of several kinds, jaspers, and jasp-agates are to be found in an area covering 1,700 acres. Free camping grounds at site. Motels and restaurants at Madras.

Mansfield of Rock, New Pine Creek, Oregon 97635. The fee is $5 per person per day. Open as early as the snow allows, and closes at the first snow in winter. The fee permits the collecting of 15 pounds of rock. All over can be purchased for 30¢ per pound.

The site contains eleven types of obsidian. The shop sells material, and is closed Wednesday. There is also a mine into which collectors may go for material, sold for less than at the shop.

Moore's Agate Acres, Route 1, Box 577, Lebanon, Oregon 97355. The beds are located 3 miles south of Lebanon on South Main Road. The fee is $3 per person per day, and there are nine digging sites. Carnelian, plume agate, banded agate, jasper, petrified wood, and other minerals are found at the locations. There is space available for campers, trailers, and tents. At the shop about 100 different kinds of materials are sold, and you may have your own finds cut and polished if desired. The sites are open from April 1 to October 1, seven days a week.

Drummond's Agate Beds, Lebanon, Oregon, on Route 2, Box 30, three miles south of town. Here you may look for carnelian and jasper, as well as for several kinds of agates. The site covers about 40 acres, and the fee is $3 per person. Camping is available, and minerals are also sold at the site. The collector is requested to bring his own tools — a shovel, pick, trowel, and rain gear if you arrive during the rainy season. The site is open from April 1 through October 15 and the collector is requested either to write or telephone Ms. Polly Drummond for a detailed map and instructions as to how to reach the diggings. You can phone from Lebanon before you go out to the house.

Valley View Mining Claims, Mr. L. Kopcinski, P.O. Box 128, Mitchell, Oregon 97750. Mr. Lopcinski operates the Lucky Strike Mine on a fee basis of 30¢ per pound for minerals taken, with the minimum of $3 per person. This is one of the best thunder-egg-collecting sites. There are rest rooms and free coffee, as well as good camping sites and spring water at the mine. Open from June through September, and in October and November by appointment, weather permitting. Seven days a week. Material is also for sale if you prefer not to dig. To reach the location, take Highway 26 east from Prineville for 31 miles to the Marks Creek Guard Station, turn left on Forest Road #127, 0.8 miles to Forest

84

Some outstanding specimens collected by my wife and me on various vacation trips.

Top row, left: *One of the finest mica "books" I have ever seen. This is a prized cabinet specimen.*

right: *A magnificant cluster of crystal selenite, from the sands of Oklahoma.*

Middle row, left: *A lovely cluster of quartz crystals, with many terminations complete — a true collector's item.*

right: *A drusy cluster of calcite from Mexico. The individual calcite crystals are covered with a rind of quartz, and the calcite fluoresces under the coating.*

Bottom row, left: *A specimen of "dog-tooth" barite. These are found in sand and in the matrix rocks of the Southwest.*

right: *A piece of rock bearing a covering of amethyst crystals, from the Thunder Bay amethyst mine in Ontario.*

Top row, left: *"Angel wing" calcite from Mexico. Parts of this cluster fluoresce, and other parts are inert.*

center: *A specimen of crystal fluorite, clearly showing the crystal habit of this important mineral.*

right: *A piece of silicon carbide, a man-made mineral better known by its trade name, Carborundum.*

Second row, left: *Orpiment (orange) and realgar, from Utah.*

center: *Chalcanthite from Mapimi, Mexico.*

right: *Limonite (ocher) and smithsonite.*

Bottom two rows: *Many of the fluorescent minerals are completely nondescript when viewed under ordinary light, but exceptionally beautiful under ultraviolet light. The bottom row shows the minerals under ultraviolet, the row above under ordinary light.*

left pair: *Calcite and willemite. Under ultraviolet the calcite is red, the willemite green.*

center pair: *Esperite and willemite. Under ultraviolet the esperite is yellow, the willemite green.*

right pair: *Calcite, esperite, and willemite. The glowing, vivid colors are extremely difficult to catch on photographic film.*

Road #123. Turn right on this road for 11.2 miles to Forest Road #125, where you turn left and follow the signs for 2 miles to the Lucky Strike Mine.

Thunder Egg Collecting Beds, Don and Ione Robins, Powell Butte, Oregon 97753. About 5 miles south of Buchanan. The fee is 25¢ per pound for any material found, and there are ten different beds opened at present. The beds are open from April 1 to October 31, and there is space available for self-contained trailers and campers, with camping sites located 5 miles away at Buchanan Station. Minerals are also sold at the sites.

Tennessee

Silvertooth Agate Field, Mr. Vaughn J. Silvertooth, Route 2, Wartrace, Tennessee 37183. The fee is $2 per person with a 10-pound limit. Over 10 pounds are charged for at the rate of 25¢ per pound. Free camping area for self-contained campers, and space for other types is available about 5 miles away. The site is open all year, seven days a week, and Mr. Silvertooth also sells agates at the site. To get to the field take Route 64 northeast from Shelbyville to Wartrace. The fields and shop are a little before you reach the town. It might be a good idea to phone to make sure he is there.

Texas

Woodward Ranch, Terlingua Route 1, Alpine, Texas 79831. An old fee-collecting site where red-flame and plume agates are to be found. The ranch is open seven days a week all year, and there are rest rooms and trailer hook-ups. The fee is 25¢ per pound for minerals dug or gathered, and agate cutting material is also sold at the ranch. Crystals, amethyst and geodes are also found there.

Bessie Mikus, Calliham, Texas, 78007. Mrs. Mikus permits collecting of agates and petrified woods on her property for the sliding fee of $2.50 to $5. She did not explain the differences in the fees. To get to her place, take Highway 281 to Three Rivers, Texas, then Highway 72 west for 12 miles to Calliham, where "everybody knows Mrs. Mikus." Camping is available and the site is open all year except during the game-hunting season.

Singing Hills Ranch, M. S. Rodriguez, c/o ABC Music Store, 1002 Hidalgo Street, Laredo, Texas 78040. A small fee provides camping space at the ranch, but there are no facilities or water available to campers. Agates, petrified woods and jasper are found on the site, which is located 5 miles west of the International Airport.

Mamie's Rock Haven, Route 1, Box 3, Falls City, Texas 78113. Mrs. Mamie Erdmann acts as a guide for the fee of $10 per day to her digging site, which has agates, petrified woods, geodes and dendrites. She is well known in Falls City, and her instructions are to ask any businessman in the city for her location upon arrival at Falls City, or to telephone her. She lives one mile east of town on the Cestohowa Road. Her site is open all winter from October through April, and she prefers a week's advance notice of your coming to collect on her property. She sells material, and there is camping space available. Falls City is about 35 miles southeast of San Antonio.

The Ernest Lange Ranch, Mason, Texas 76856. A topaz-collecting site. The fee is $3 per person per day. Camping space is available at the site, and the diggings are open 365 days of the year. According to instructions, you drive from Mason west for 8.3 miles on Route 377 to a ranch road, turning left on that road for 1.2 miles to the entrance. It might be good to call from Mason to get more detailed directions.

Seaquist Honey Creek Ranch, Garner E. Seaquist, 401 Broad Street, Mason, Texas 76856. For a fee of $5 per day per person one may hunt for smoky quartz, topaz, and other minerals. Excellent camping and trailer area on the ranch, as well as air-conditioned cabin with kitchenette. The site is open 365 days of the year. You must go to the Seaquist home at the address given above for your permit and key to the ranch gate.

Bob's Knob, Zapata, Texas 78076. This seems to be a perhaps unique collecting site, since apparently you collect your agate, jasper, and petrified wood from a boat! The collecting site is situated on the Falcon Reservoir, and you collect at low tide. The fee is $1 per person and there are camp grounds at the site. Drive 13 miles south of Zapata on Highway 83, then turn right on a gravel road for 9 miles to the site. Signs mark the way.

Davenport Ranch, Mrs. Wesley Loeffler, Grit, Texas 76846. Drive 5 miles west from Mason, Texas, on Highway 29 — called the Menard Highway. The office and Mrs. Loeffler are at the Grit General Store and Post Office. Fee is $5 per person per day. In groups of ten or more, the fee is $3 per person. Topaz and smoky quartz are found at this site. Camping near the area and pasture camping permitted for longer stays. Open from January 2 to November 1. Closed Sunday and sometimes Saturday afternoons.

Joe Tom Bishop, P.O. Box 201, Marfa, Texas 79843 located on Highway 169 a few miles south of Marfa; and E. K. Beanland, P.O. Box 745, Marfa, Texas 79843 located on State Highway 67 a few miles south of Marfa. These two ranches are fee-collecting sites, charging $6 per day per person, permitting the collecting of 20 pounds of material. All material over the initial 20 pounds is charged for at the rate of 30¢ per pound. Camping is available, but no utilities. The ranches are open all year except from mid-November through mid-December. Bouquet, banded pastel, and plume agates are to be found, and plain opal. The owners request that you call them from Marfa before going to the ranches. Trespassers are prosecuted, so permission must be obtained.

Stillwell Trailer Camp. Located 46 miles south of Marathon, off U.S. 385; take farm road 2627 east for 6 miles to the camp. The fee is 35¢ per pound. On the site are agates and petrified wood.

Open all year every day of the week. The automobile maps published by Texaco show the Stillwell Ranch, located near the Mexican border. Camping facilities available, as the name indicates.

Virginia

Morefield Beryl Mines, Mr. Deck R. Boyles, Route 4, Box 307, Amelia, Virginia 23002. Mr. Boyles operates two mines; the fee is $1 per person per day for each mine. You must go to the address above for a permit and information. From Amelia, take Highway 360 northeast to State Road 628, where you turn right for 1½ miles to the first two-story white house on the left. The mailbox is marked D. R. Boyles, #307. Beryl, smoky quartz, mica books, topaz, garnet, tourmaline, moonstone, agate and many more minerals are found in the mines. The sites are open all year, and campsites are nearby.

Mica Mine Farm, O. W. Harris, Route 2, Box 137, Beaver Dam, Virginia 23015. Here you may collect moonstone, garnet, kyanite, amazonite, mica, etc., for a fee of $1 per day, 75¢ for children under 12. Bring your own digging tools. The Shady Grove Motel is 10 miles from the mine. Picnic grounds are available at the site. The mine is open all year, every day. The owner informs me that a new Disney World is being constructed at Daswell, 10 miles from the mine, with camping sites, motels, etc.

Washington

Fran and Ollie's Rock and Gem Shop, 123 First Avenue, Okanogan, Washington 98840. Eighteen or twenty different minerals are to be found around this area, and the above rock shop will give information, or get permission and directions for collectors wishing to go on field trips. The Okanogan Chamber of Commerce, located at the same address as the rock shop, will mail you a map of the area showing camping sites, ranger stations, etc. The fees vary in the different sites.

Canada

Gerry McCoy, Quadville, Ontario, Canada. Take the Canada
Highway 401 to Napanee, then north on Highway #41 to Denbigh, (about 69 miles); east from Denbigh on Highway #500 to
Hardwood Lake Store, then north on Highway #515 to Quadville. Once there, you should telephone Mr. McCoy for further
instructions. His diggings are just before Quadville on Highway
515. For the fee of 50¢ per pound you may dig in his rose-quartz
mine, and for the fee of $2 per person you may collect at his peg-
matite quarry, where many prize minerals are available, including beryl, tourmaline, fluorite, amazonite and many others.
The fee includes a guide, and identification of any minerals you
find. Camping sites are available at the sites, which are open
seven days a week from mid-May through October.

Dave Woodcox Farm, Tory Hill, Ontario, Postal 9, Kolzyo. This is
a site where many different minerals can be collected for the fee
of $1 per adult, and 50¢ for children. Camping is available near
the site, which is open seven days a week all year. Tory Hill is
about 50 miles almost due north of Petersborough on Route 507.

Thunder Bay Amethyst Mines. Near the center of the North shore
of Lake Superior is located an entire mountain of amethyst. The
Thunder Bay Amethyst Mines are open to the public from May 1
to November 1, seven days a week. For a fee of 35¢ per pound
you may pick up amethyst that has been bulldozed or blasted
from the mines. Camping areas are about 10 miles from the mine,
which is reached by driving east from Thunder Bay on the Trans-
Canada Highway 17 to East Loon Road, then turning north on
that road and following the signs to the mine, which is located
on the top of the mountain. The road is pretty bad, so do not attempt to take a trailer up. There are parking places at the bottom
of the road where you may unhitch and proceed in your car.
There is a shop where prize specimens of amethyst are sold at
reasonable prices.

The open-pit amethyst mine at Thunder Bay, Ontario. A marvelous place to go for beautiful specimens.

6.

Preparation
and Display of Specimens

Minerals and rocks improperly displayed or haphazardly stored are merely an accumulation of dust-gathering nuisances. When properly prepared, they make a collection of great beauty and interest. As with nearly everything in the area of natural history and ecology, a collection of minerals must be properly labeled and identified in order to have any value or usefulness. It simply is not enough to have a hunk of rock and explain it thus: "I think this is chalcedony, but it may be selenium. We found it in Montana, or was it Utah? Maybe we got it on our trip through Arizona." This lack of information and identification makes an otherwise valuable mineral specimen just another rock that might as well have been left in the ground where it was found.

It is true that if you purchase specimens from a dealer, the collecting data may be sketchy. The answer to this, unless the specimen is really outstanding and very rare, is to leave it at the dealer's and look elsewhere for your specimen. However, if a mineral specimen *is* rare and outstanding, the dealer is almost certain to have the pertinent information on it.

If you have no other way to keep track of minerals on a field trip, the best and simplest way to provide information is to wrap each specimen in a paper towel, or even a sheet of old newspaper, taking care that the entire specimen is covered. With the chunk, wrap a small piece of paper giving the location, date, finder, and—if you are able to do so in the fields—the identification of the specimen. This will enable you to keep the data applicable to that particular specimen *with* the specimen until such time as you are ready to make the permanent label and entry in your catalog, no matter how much time elapses before you get around to it.

CLEANING OF SPECIMENS

Rocks and mineral specimens must undergo certain treatment before they are ready to be put into a collection or placed on display. First, they must be cleaned to permit evaluation. Often a

A septarian nodule sliced in half to show the inside. When polished a nodule makes a valuable cabinet specimen.

chunk which looks promising in the field will turn out to be so gross and in such poor condition that it is better left out of your display. This determination is best made after the material has been cleaned.

The first stage of cleaning may be done in the yard with your garden hose or, if you are an apartment dweller, in the kitchen sink. The sink has two disadvantages, however. One is the lack of force from the faucet, and the other is that the washed-away dirt and clay might clog the drain. If the specimen has an inordinate amount of clinging soil and clay, it is best to brush away as much of the foreign material as possible before washing off the remainder. Of course you must use some judgment when cleaning material. Very soft, fragile and delicate specimens can neither be washed nor brushed without the real danger of ruining the material. Some of the forms of calcite, for example, are so fragile that even handling them will fracture away bits every time they are touched. "Velvet" malachite and many other minerals which form needlelike crystals sometimes thinner than a hair are so fragile that they cannot be touched at all. Even blowing on them to remove foreign matter will possibly distort or fracture the fine mass of needles or hairs. These minerals, fortunately, are found as linings in vugs and cavities, and are usually clean in nature. Your job, then, if you find any of them, is to keep them clean and free from physical damage while transporting them home to your collection. They cannot be wrapped, so the best way is to glue them to the styrofoam bottom of a plastic specimen box, removing them later, if you desire, after they are safely home.

Also, one thing to remember is that some minerals are soluble in water, and it stands to reason that these, too, may not be washed without ruining them. I have a most beautiful and dramatic specimen of chalcanthite that was ruined by being washed in water. The sharp edges of all the individual crystals have been melted away, leaving them rounded, and the matrix rock, upon which the crystals formed, is stained blue.

After the first cleaning, each specimen should be put aside to dry naturally, not dried with a cloth, since this action may leave lint all over the piece, or even break off sharp and delicate points of small crystals. The label you made in the field when collecting the specimen should be kept with that piece all through these operations. It is not a good idea, if you have several specimens of different minerals, to try to remember which is which. The label is a much surer way of keeping the identification accurate.

When the specimen has dried thoroughly, you may again examine it to make sure that all extraneous dirt has been removed. If there was a lot of clay present, this may not have been removed by the first washing. Clay is very difficult to dissolve by immersion in water, and when it gets wet it expands. This merely tightens the clay in the crevices of the mineral. After the specimen has dried, however, you will see that any particles of clay remaining on and in it will have shrunk to the point where they can be easily picked out with a needle, ice pick, knitting needle, or some similar tool. If the mineral being cleaned is sturdy, you can often brush out pockets of clay with a stiff brush, or even a wire brush if the mineral is very hard.

Thin crusts of foreign materials may be removed from the faces of crystals with the aid of dental tools. Every dentist has some tools which are too worn for further dental use, and he will be glad to let you have them for cleaning minerals. The worn tools are excellent for prying loose layers of disfiguring material, picking out small flakes of foreign minerals, and for general cleaning-up of a specimen. Naturally, these tools should be used with great care on any mineral soft enough to be scratched with a knife. On harder minerals there is little danger of spoiling the surface with a scratch from a dental instrument.

Acid Cleaning

Sometimes a specimen will be stained with iron and rustlike discolorations, which simple washing and scrubbing will fail to remove. These tenacious stains can be removed in an acid bath, but be very careful to avoid burning your own skin. Oxalic acid can be used in the proportion of 8 ounces of the dry powdered acid to 1 gallon of water. Stains which will not disappear in a hot oxalic acid bath might be removed by using hydrochloric acid diluted one-part acid to two-parts water. Always add the acid to the water when diluting. Never pour water into acid! The commercial product called *muriatic acid,* which is sold in paint and hardware stores, is an impure grade of hydrochloric acid about the strength used for cleaning minerals. Use this as it comes from the bottle. For minerals belonging to the carbonate family, the acid should be diluted even further, say about 1 part acid to 15 or 20 parts of water. Acid baths work better when warm. They should be used as hot as you can stand, but not boiling.

Rubber gloves should be worn to avoid skin burns, and the eyes should be protected against splashes by goggles. Avoid inhaling the fumes of any acid as you work; some of them can be quite corrosive to lung tissue. Always use acid baths in a well-ventilated area, and make sure that the bath is on a steady support so it will not tip over accidentally.

PROTECTION FROM ATMOSPHERE AND LIGHT

Many minerals are destroyed by exposure to the atmosphere. Unless it is protected in some manner, the specimen will, in time, disintegrate into powder or, at the very least, the entire surface will oxidize to the point where the true nature of the mineral is obscured. Ulexite is an example of the latter progess, and marcasite will, in time, alter to another mineral, melanterite, and the specimen will slowly crumble into whitish powder until all the marcasite is gone.

One method of protecting such oxidizable minerals is to wash them in alcohol, then in an ammonia bath, dry them thoroughly, then spray with a clear lacquer. Several coats should be sprayed on the specimen, taking care to see that every bit of the surface is sealed with the lacquer.

Certain minerals are so sensitive to light that they fade or even change color after continued exposure. These are best kept in drawers, or perhaps in boxes made of an opaque material rather than plastic boxes, and replaced in their dark containers immediately after viewing. It is a good practice not to view such sensitive minerals in a strong light, but rather in subdued lighting, preferably under artificial illumination rather than in sunlight. Sunlight works much faster upon light-sensitive materials than does incandescent light, and the action of prolonged exposure to the ultraviolet rays in sunlight can do some strange and damaging things to certain minerals.

GRADING OF SPECIMENS

After the minerals are thoroughly dried, they may be examined for the best way to trim them, if they need trimming. The preparation of specimens takes some time and care, but the results are well worth the effort. As a matter of fact, a collection of random sizes and shapes of rocks and minerals does not do very much to enhance their beauty or value. It is a good idea to decide upon one kind of collection, and grade the sizes of your specimens to fall within that category. An exception is a museum collection, in which the individual specimens are kept as large as possible and, usually, in just the condition in which they were found.

In a study collection, school collection, or home collection, however, it is the usual practice to grade each piece to within a certain size. The popular sizes are: school specimen, approximately 1 × 2 inches in size, which sizes are also sometimes called study collections; cabinet specimens, which are about 3 × 4 inches; and display specimens, from cabinet size up to about 6 × 6 inches and sometimes a little larger. Descending to smaller sizes, we have the "thumbnail" collection, in which the specimens are only rarely larger than 1 inch in any direction; and the micromounts collection, in which very small specimens are individually mounted on a support of some kind inside a small plastic box about 1 × 1 × 1 inch in size. Some of these boxes have a lens molded into the top to magnify the contents. A micromount collection is necessarily viewed through a magnifying lens of some kind. For casual viewing, larger pieces are far easier to manage and view, but micromounts and thumbnails have the advantage of comparatively small cost per specimen if you are purchasing them. They enable you to own rare and valuable minerals which, in a cabinet size, might cost several hundreds of dollars. It is also easier to obtain perfect crystals and clusters of crystals in these smaller sizes than in the larger sizes. Mounting procedures are discussed later in this chapter.

Micromounts have rare beauty in spite of their extremely small size. In a great many "coffee-table" books on minerals, you will note that most of the specimens pictured, while they may occupy a full page, are really only a millimeter or two across. The enlargement needed to present them in the photograph does nothing detrimental to the appearance of the specimen. Usually, the true size of a specimen is noted in the caption accompanying the photograph.

TRIMMING OF SPECIMENS

Trimming can be done by hand, with a hammer and a cold chisel. Or, if you intend doing a lot of this work, you can invest in the reasonably small cost of a trimming machine. This device has a pair of chisel jaws that are brought together by means of a powerful screw. The specimen is placed between the jaws and the screw tightened until the material snaps off. When using the trimmer, either wear goggles or turn your face aside as you tighten the screw to avoid having a chip fly into your eye. Usually no chips break loose, but there is always that possibility, so it is wiser to take precautions. Trimmers can be made with a hydraulic automobile jack, too, and these are very useful for large specimens that would be beyond the power of the screw-post trimmer. If you are handy mechanically and have access to a machine shop, you could put together a trimmer yourself.

The reason for trimming, as mentioned, is to size specimens uniformly. A second reason is that by trimming, all base rock can be removed from a specimen, most especially if it is a drusy coating on the matrix rock. In some cases not *all* the base rock is removed, but just the portions interfering with easy viewing of

A rock splitter, used to trim specimens to better size and shape.

the important material. Also, the specimen can be trimmed in such a manner as to provide a base for support on a shelf, permitting the specimen to rest steady without tipping. When trimming specimens with a cold chisel and hammer, the use of a sand box will simplify your task. This is nothing more than a stout wooden box about a foot square and of the same depth, filled with about 10 inches of sand. The sand should be dampened when working specimens. A piece of the mineral being trimmed is bedded into the damp sand. Holding the chisel firmly in place on the line you wish to trim, strike it with a hard blow of the hammer. One strike should snap off that section, and the chisel is moved on down the line, cracking off a short section with each blow. If more than one blow is needed to break the mineral, take care that the chisel is held in precisely the same spot for each successive blow, to make an even break. The sand cushions the shock of the hammer blows and keeps the specimen from shattering as the edge is snapped away. By turning the specimen around, you can trim each side. After a few specimens have been trimmed, you will find the work easy and fast.

Small specimens can be trimmed with a tile cutter. These are sturdy nippers which have jaws tipped with tungsten carbide, and which do not close all the way. They are intended to snap off pieces of ceramic tiles used for bathroom floors and walls, and are obtainable from companies which deal in tile for construction purposes. If no tile company is near your home, Sears, Roebuck and Company lists them in their catalog under the name *Tile Cutting Nippers*. I have a pair which has been in use for over three years, and the carbide jaws are still true and sharp, since tungsten carbide is harder than any mineral or rock except diamond.

THUMBNAILS AND MICROMOUNTS

Thumbnails and micromounts usually do not have to be trimmed unless they are being made from large pieces of material. Thumbnail specimens are also usually mounted in the small plastic boxes mentioned earlier, on a piece of styrofoam cut to fit into the bottom of the box. A drop of adhesive holds the mineral in place, if you do not intend to handle the specimens very much, or will not want to take them out of the boxes for closer examination. Otherwise, it is better not to glue the specimen fast, or at least to cut the styrofoam to a size that will permit easy insertion and removal from the box.

In the case of micromounts, some kind of pedestal must be used to support the specimen, and, bearing in mind that often the specimen will be no larger than the head of a pin—if even that large—the pedestal must be sized in proportion. As a matter of fact, pins make good pedestals, especially if the head is turned down a bit smaller. This turning can be done with a file, holding the pin and rotating it in the fingers as you file away the surplus metal, or the pin can be chucked in a hand drill and turned with that machine while holding the head against a file or a piece of emery cloth. Whatever way you turn the heads down, enough material should be left to make a tiny platform by touching the top of the head with the file to flatten it.

For larger micromount specimens short pieces of glass or plastic rods will make excellent pedestals. The rods should be not more than ⅛ inch in diameter for specimens up to, say 8 or 10 millimeters across. Glass rods may be cut by nicking them with a three-cornered file at the point desired, then snapping the rod with the fingers. It should break off cleanly. If you first wrap the rod in a paper napkin, any chip flying off will be caught. Also sections of aluminum tubing, such as those sold in hobby stores for model building, will work very well. For the very largest in the micromount category, golf tees serve as good pedestals. The heads may have to be sanded down a bit, but otherwise the tee should serve admirably.

When setting up a micromount, you must necessarily perform the work under a magnifying glass. Because of the very small size of the specimen, a glass should be not less than 10-power. It should not be much stronger, though, because the stronger the magnification, the more difficult it is to work under it.

An excellent glue to use for fastening specimens to pedestals is the white glue commonly sold in all hardware stores today. The advantage of this glue is that it will adhere to both the specimen and the pinhead very well, but if you ever want to remove the mineral from the mount for any reason, it is easy to do so by immersing the whole in warm water for a few minutes to dissolve the glue.

STORING SPECIMENS

Neat, uniform, easily cleaned plastic trays are manufactured by Ward's Natural Science Establishment Inc., of Rochester, New York, for the storage of mineral specimens. They are reasonably priced. They fit inside shallow drawers of specimen cabinets (although they will also fit inside ordinary drawers), and each tray has a shelf in front upon which an adhesive label may be attached. The trays are made in three sizes, for the three most popular-sized specimens. Trays having 45 compartments and boxes having 50 compartments are also available for collections of thumbnail specimens.

Trays or boxes of some kind or another should always be used in storing a collection of mineral specimens, to keep the specimens from hitting and rubbing against one another. While you might think that touching each other should not injure hard rocks, still there is a good possibility that one will rub a streak off on another specimen. This streak will show the color of one mineral on another mineral and may be next to impossible to remove.

CATALOGING SPECIMENS

Having washed and trimmed your specimens, you are now ready to make your permanent record of the data concerning each individual item. About the best way to maintain data in a mineral collection is to use a small notebook in which all entries can be made under a numbering system. On the specimen itself, a small area is selected in an inconspicuous place, usually on the back or on the bottom, and this area is painted white with a good grade of house paint, such as a matte surface paint. The area need be no larger than about $1/4 \times 1/2$ inch in size, because all you are going to put in the space is a number.

Having painted your specimens, you may now paint or write a number on the painted area, using either a fine brush and India ink, or a pen point with the same ink. Use the waterproof kind, and be sure to make the number clear and legible.

As soon as each number is put on a specimen, enter that number in the notebook, and after it all the collecting data you have for it. Its identification is also put in the book, either as you number them, if they have been identified, or as soon as identification is made. The number will in any event serve to keep all the information for that particular specimen at your convenience.

After the specimens are all prepared and placed in their permanent place in either a drawer or a cabinet shelf, you may, if you wish, use individual labels under the specimen. This way you will not have to try to remember every single item in your collection—a difficult job if the collection is very extensive—but as you look at, or show the specimens, you can identify them by the individual labels.

II.

FROM ROCKS AND MINERALS TO GEMS AND JEWELRY

7.

Tumbling Stones

When the craft of gem cutting became popular a few years ago, the first treatment available was tumble polishing. This started out as a hobby craft, rather than as a part of lapidary work, and the use of tumble-polished stones rapidly became a major fad. It still is.

Every lapidary shop should have a tumbler, because in the course of cutting gemstones you will have a lot of scrap material, which can be tumbled and used in many different ways, as articles of jewelry and in other crafts.

Almost every hobbyshop and department store now sells tumbling machines and complete kits containing the machine, abrasive powders, and a bag of tumbling rough to start you off. Rock shops and mail-order houses sell tumbling rough, which is cutting material broken into small pieces suitable for producing polished freeform gems. This material is sold by the pound, and is quite cheap. It is available as mixed stones and in bags containing only one kind of stone: various agates, amethyst, jasper, or other kinds.

Tumbling is a simple operation. It merely takes time. The machine consists of two rods, revolving in bearings. One rod is driven by a motor. The other acts as an idler and guide for the drum, which is a metal sheath containing a rubber barrel shaped like a pentagon, hexagon, octagon, or just plain round. Essentially the process consists of placing the rocks, abrasive, and water in the drum and sealing it, then rotating it in the machine for a given period of time. The stones, tumbling about inside the drum with the mixture of abrasive and water, wear their surfaces smooth. With progressively finer abrasives and, finally, a polishing compound, an amazingly perfect polish is obtained on the fragmented minerals.

Tumblers are available in a variety of sizes and styles. All depend on the action of abrasive powders against the stones. A useful size for the hobbyist is one having a drum that will hold about three pounds of rocks. This size also comes double. That is, the steel drum holds two three-pound rubber drums, each one individually sealed. The convenience of a double drum is that if you have a lot of material to tumble, one load may be started in one drum. Then, when that load is ready for the second stage — that is, a finer abrasive — you can start another batch on its first stage in that drum and put the first load in the other drum with second-stage abrasive. When the third stage is required for the first load, it can be put aside, and the second load can be put into the second-stage drum. The first stage drum is cleaned and charged with third-stage abrasive. This way you save one tumbling time for each load all the way through the process.

Each time the grit is changed in the drum, the drum and the stones must be thoroughly cleaned of the previous grit. Not one grain of grit should remain when you recharge the drums with the next finer step.

A tumbler should be set up in a spot where it is out of the way and still convenient to reach. Since the tumbling process takes several weeks, and the machine must run twenty-four hours a day, don't set it in operation in a place you may need for other work. On the floor in a corner, on a lower shelf of a workbench, or even up on a shelf — any place where it can be left to run for the required length of time without interfering with your other activities.

Tumbling grits are sold in sets of cans, each can supplying enough grit for a large load. In a three-pound drum, each can will supply enough material to tumble two full loads. The best tumbling action is obtained with four-stage grits. These are three grinding grades and one polishing grade, or two grinding grits, one pre-polishing grit, and one polish. Stones can be tumbled in three stages, but I do not recommend that, since so much better results are obtained with the one extra step.

If you use bulk grit, then the first grit should be 100 mesh, the second stage 220 mesh, and the third stage 400 mesh. You will have even better results if you go to a fourth abrasive grade of 600 grit. Tin oxide is used for the polish. Another system is to start with 220 grit, running this a little longer than normal, then 400, 600, and the polish, eliminating the first very coarse 100-grit step.

A three-pound load should take about a full cup of abrasive powder. Then fill the drum with just enough water to cover the stones. Seal the drum well to eliminate any spillage, and place it on the rods of the machine. Tumble twenty-four hours a day for six days, if you are using 100 grit as the first step, or eight days if you are using the 220 grit at first.

It is a good idea to stop the drum and open it every other day. This is not to examine the progress of the tumbling, but to let out any gases that accumulate within the drum. While it is not really a hazard, drums have been known to explode when the gas released by the minerals during the tumbling action builds up inside the drum. The opening of the drums will completely eliminate this danger.

After each grind, the drum and the stones should be thoroughly cleaned of every grain of abrasive. The drums are easy to wash, as are their covers. However, some of the stones may prove more difficult, especially if they have any holes or crevices in them to catch and hold the grit. These holes must be washed free of every grain of powder before entering the next stage of tumbling. A fine spray, toothpicks, ice pick, or other picking tool can be used. An old toothbrush is also very convenient for brushing away the abrasive which seems to cling with magnetic force to the inner recesses of voids in stones. This is because they are usually lined with very fine drusy crystals that hold any foreign matter.

The best way to wash a load of stones is to tip them out of the drum into a colander, and wash under running water until the water runs clear. Then each stone is picked out of the colander and rinsed off in another pan of clean water, first examining it to see if there are any holes or cavities. The ones with these surface irregularities are put aside for further cleaning. All the other stones can be placed back in the drum to await the start of the new stage. Now the irregulars may be brushed, sprayed, or whatever you must do to make certain they are perfectly clean. Then add them to the drum, with the new charge of abrasive powder and water, and close up for tumbling.

In the polish stage about one cupful of plastic tumbling pellets is added to the drum. These add to the rubbing action against the stones, and distribute the polish evenly throughout the charge in the drum. They also soften the impact of the stones against each other, which, in the final stage, might chip or nick some of the softer pieces.

Plastic tumbling pellets may be purchased wherever you get your abrasive powders, and the pellets may be used over and over again.

After the polishing stage is completed, the stones and drum are again washed thoroughly. Then the stones are returned to the drum, covered with water and a clean cupful of plastic pellets, together with a tablespoonful of powdered detergent, or about $1/4$ cupful of liquid detergent. They are tumbled for about two hours. This will remove all the film left by the polishing compound and brighten the surface of the stones, which now should be mirror-polished. The stones are washed and dried in sawdust or in an old terrycloth towel. You will find many uses for them in the making of jewelry.

Tumbling Beads

Tumble-polishing beads is a slightly different thing from polishing stones. About the most important thing is to omit the first, or coarse grinding, stage, since the beads, in being sized and shaped in the bead mill, have already gone through that stage.

Instead, you start right off with the 220-mesh powder, and tumble for about two days, then examine a bead or two to see if all the coarse mill scratches are gone. If any of the coarse scratches show, return the beads to the mill and grind for another two days.

Perform the same operation with every grind, examining after two days of constant tumbling. In the final polishing stage the tumbler should run for the full period of time. Do not forget to include the cupful of plastic tumbling pellets.

If, in polishing beads, you have much less than a full load for the drum, you may add a partial load of small pieces of stone of almost any kind to make up the deficiency. A drum will not grind or polish well unless it has a full load. A method which has met with some success is to keep a box of small rounded waterworn pebbles from a pebble beach or riverbank in the cutting room and use these pebbles as fillers when polishing beads. The pebbles can be sorted out to match most nearly the size of the beads, and they can be used many times before they are ground down so far as to be useless. Almost any stream or river, and some lakes, will have places full of such waterworn pebbles, and you can grade out a large boxful in a matter of a few minutes.

Tumbling Odd-Shaped Stones and Softer Stones

Odd shapes of cut gems can also be tumble-polished to advantage. Sometimes the shape prevents polishing or even smoothing out in preparation for the polish. These items are easily polished in the tumbler, and the same system of grinds and polishing as used for regular stone fragments should be followed. It is difficult to understand, but minerals with very delicate sections can go through the various stages of tumble polishing without fracturing or cracking into pieces.

However, it is not good practice to mix stones in the same load having a radically different hardness. If, for example, a load of agates had a few pieces of malachite or rhodochrosite mixed with it, you would probably find at the end of the tumbling cycle that the latter two gems had completely disappeared! The softer material will be ground away and become part of the slurry in the drum, the action much hastened by the hard agates tumbling against them. As a matter of fact, soft stones cannot be tumbled to any degree of success if you are trying to maintain a certain size in the pieces. They grind away at an alarming rate under the coarser stages, and even the pre-polishing stage will remove more material than you think possible.

The same is true of pieces of obsidian. Although they are fairly hard, they grind very readily, and fragments placed in a tumbler will come out with a mirror finish, usually, but also only about half the size they were when they went into the machine. After tumbling a load or two of this kind of material, you will learn just how long it takes for the polish to be achieved, as well as the length of time each grinding stage should be given, and a record can be kept for future reference. Each person will have an individual way of doing something that will mean slight variations in the techniques, the time required, and the results achieved.

8.

Tools and Equipment
for Gem Making

Any art form or craft requires special materials, tools, and equipment in order to perform the various steps in creating an object in that medium. Gem cutting is no exception. Certain machines are essential, and their use must be mastered before you can really turn out gemstones without fear of ruining the work in one stage or another. Mastering of gem-making equipment is, fortunately, most easy and takes very little time and practice.

The simplest machine is, of course, the tumbler, discussed in the preceding chapter. Although tumbled stones are in a sense novelties rather than works of art, tumbling is deservedly popular both as an easy technique for beginners and as a method for utilizing scraps of stones from more ambitious gem-making projects.

In this chapter I am listing tools and equipment essential for a well-equipped gem-making shop. By "shop" I do not mean a commercial shop, but your own hobby shop. With the equipment discussed here, you will be able to turn out every conceivable kind of cabochon stone, spheres, slabs, specimen pieces, and displays. At the end of the chapter is a listing of manufacturers and suppliers of the equipment discussed.

113

Saws

The first machine every gem cutter must have is a saw. Actually, the complete hobby shop needs three saws, and if you work with precious material such as opal, you will need a fourth. The slabbing saw is one with as large a blade as your space and pocketbook can afford. The kit-type saws made by Duc-Kit are ideal as far as operation goes, and they are about a sixth the cost of a ready-assembled machine. This slabbing saw will take care of the large chunks of minerals you either dig yourself or purchase as cutting rough from rock shops.

Next, you need a small slab saw. This one could be about a 10-inch size, such as the Lortone saw illustrated in the next chapter. The advantage of this particular size and model is that it is self-contained, has a power feed, and takes the small pieces of mineral that cannot be cut on the large slabber. It can also, in a pinch, be used as a trim saw, but I prefer an overhead type for this critical cutting. The Lortone saw uses a sump instead of a coolant pump. The blade dips into the coolant in the sump, carrying it up and throwing it on the work as the machine runs.

The trim saw can be smaller than the small slabbing saw. An 8-inch trim saw is large enough for almost anything you can do in a gem shop. The Preformer saw in my shop is made by H.O.P.E. in Riverside, California. The blade is mounted on an arm which is pivoted at the rear. The motor is also mounted on the rear of the arm and acts as a counterbalance for the blade and arbor. While the machine is equipped with a pump which recirculates the coolant in the sump built into the base of the saw, I have hooked mine up to the water supply which feeds all my machines except the 20-inch and 10-inch slab saws. With the Preformer saw you can see the work right at the place of cutting, so you can trim your blanks as closely as desired. It is handy for making several pieces the same size and shape when you use the two cutting guides supplied as standard with the machine.

If you work opal or go into faceting—which is not discussed in this book—you will certainly need a thin-kerf slitting saw. These saws use a diamond blade that is a great deal thinner than a regular one of the same size, and in use takes considerably less of the material away when it slits the rough into smaller pieces for working into the individual gems. Since rare-gem material is sold by the carat or the gram, you can lose a lot of money just by the saw kerf if you do not cut them on a thin-kerf blade. Thin blades must run at appreciably greater speeds than regular blades. Raytech makes a thin-kerf slitting saw that works very well for slitting precious material. It has a 6-inch-diameter blade and a power-feed carriage. The blade runs in a sump, picking up the coolant and carring it to the work as it runs. The sump is easily emptied and cleaned in this saw, since the entire table lifts up off the sump, exposing it for servicing.

Sanders

The tool most important after the diamond saw is the sander. Sanding is done either on a disc covered with the proper abrasive sheet or on a drum with an abrasive belt against which the stone is held and rotated while the belt is running, water being fed to the belt constantly to keep the stone cool and to wash away any collected dust and grindings. Pfizer Minerals produces Ultralap discs, which are abrasives and polishes coated on thin plastic sheet. The discs are designed to be cemented to the rubber-backed metal discs supplied with the Ray-Tilt machine mentioned below, and on discs of other machines. They are excellent for the final stages of gem polishing. If you are using abrasive belts for the first and second sanding stages, the stone can be brought to a perfect finish and even polished on the Ultralaps. Several different polishing compounds are provided for polishing various types of gem materials.

Raytech makes the Ray-Tilt, a complete gem-maker unit in itself. This machine is supplied with a 6 × 1-inch gem-grinding wheel, several rubber-faced discs, and a few plastic Ultralap discs of different surfaces and grades. All operations from grinding to polishing cabochons may be performed on the Ray-Tilt machine, and, if you are polishing only an occasional stone, this machine with a slab and trim saw would do the job capably.

A selection of gems cut from minerals collected on field trips.

Left column, top to bottom: *Sagenitic agate (California)*
Twin Creeks jasper (Wyoming)
Orbicular jasper (California)
Plume agate (Montana)
Queen jasper (Nevada)

Center column: *Lace agate (Mexico)*
Laguna agate (Mexico)
Mahogany obsidian (Yellowstone
National Park)
Rhodochrosite (South America)
Graveyard Point agate (Idaho)
Lace Agate (Mexico)
Onyx (Mexico)

Right column: *Petrified mahogany (Eden Valley,*
Wyoming)
Howlite (California)
Lace agate (Oregon)
Petrified oak (Oregon)
Rutilated quartz (South America)
Veil agate (Wyoming)

When does a mineral become a gem? Some are beautiful just as they come from the field, others begin to reveal their glory at an early stage of gem making such as slicing, and still others remain drab pebbles until the polishing stage, and then surrender their beauty all at once. Finally, to some collectors and cutters a stone is not a gem until it has been incorporated into an article of jewelry.

Top row, left: Slices of mineral, ready to be scribed and sawn to shape. Top to bottom: rhodonite, Mexican agate, and Brazilian agate nodule.

center: More slices. Top to bottom: snowflake obsidian, Canadian sodalite, agate from Idaho, and pink orbicular jasper.

right: Cabochons made from five consecutive slices of the same chunk of mineral. These will become a necklace.

Middle row, left: A necklace with interchangeable pendants: lace agate, mahogany obsidian, and rhodochrosite.

center: The four stones are from the same piece of mahogany obsidian, found in Wyoming.

right: Simply mounted necklace and earrings of sodalite from the Princess Mine in Ontario. Sodalite of this purity is very rare.

Bottom row, left: The individual stones, all from one slice of lace agate, were matched, then set in an articulated mounting with an Egyptian feeling.

center: A free-form slice of chrysocolla from New Mexico, tumble-polished and set in sterling.

right: A striking pendant of variscite, a mineral first discovered in Utah (now scarce from overcollecting).

The expanding-drum type of sander is my favorite because it is capable of taking diamond belts as well as abrasive belts, making the sanding so much faster and easier that it pays to use the more costly diamond items. Duc-Kit makes a kit containing the arbor, two expanding drums, and a splash pan fitted with water petcocks to feed the coolant to the top of the drums. The kit is easily assembled, and the arbor is operated by a ½-horse-power motor.

Diamond Dishes and Discs

For the shaping of cabochons, diamond dishes and discs are invaluable. It is true that cabochons can be ground on a regular abrasive wheel — or rather an abrasive wheel made for lapidary work — but the work is infinitely faster and much easier with diamond-impregnated materials. The 3M Company manufactures diamond dishes in several different grits. These can be used on the Ray-Tilt machine or on an arbor. They are excellent for shaping cabochons up to about 30 × 40-millimeter ellipses. Larger sizes are better shaped on the 3M faceting discs. These are precision discs charged with diamonds in grades from 100 mesh down to 6 micron-mesh. The last grade is of little use for cabochon work, being intended for the pre-polishing stage of faceting gemstones. However, the 100 mesh or the 220 mesh are wonderful tools for shaping large or odd-shaped cabochons, and they will last a very long time if properly used. This means using them with minimal pressure and sufficient coolant to keep the diamonds free of packed material. Water is perfectly all right to use, and if you can set up your machine with running — or rather, dripping — water, with a drain of some kind, you are all set to grind large stones.

Polishers

Polishing is done on laps covered with a variety of materials. Duc-Kit makes a polishing-lap kit that is excellent for this part of cabochon cutting. The laps are threaded onto a vertical arbor running inside a splash pan, and each lap can be covered as you desire. Canvas covers are supplied which have drawstrings in them to pull the material tightly around the lap, and a cushion of foam rubber is used under the canvas as a pressure surface. Leather, felt, and Pellon cloth can all be used on the laps, depending on what kind of stone you are working. (Pellon cloth is a felt-like material used in tailoring for linings; it is available in fabrics stores.)

Other Equipment

The saws, grinder, sander, and polisher are the main pieces of equipment needed for producing cabochons. For other work, such as sphere-making, slab and geode polishing, different ma-

The Lortone 20-inch vibrating lap in operation, polishing a load of slabs. Lead weights fastened to a slab with dopping cement will help the action of the lap.

A sphere being polished in one of the Bernstein sphere-making machines. Note the adjustment of tension on the heads by the use of rubber bands.

chines are used. Lortone manufactures a reasonably priced vibrating lap for polishing slabs, large blocks for book-ends, geode halves, and similar projects. This machine can be started and the work is automatic; all you have to do is make sure there is enough water and grit in the lap, while you go about other work.

Mr. Alfred Bernstein has designed a sphere-making machine which is very ingenious and very reasonable in cost. In it perfect spheres can easily be ground. In the chapter on spheres, this work will be discussed at greater length.

Other tools, materials, and supplies will be discussed in their proper place in this book, as the processes employing them are explained.

MANUFACTURERS AND SUPPLIERS

There are many manufacturers whose products I have not tested myself, and so I have not listed them here. They all advertise their products in the periodicals listed in Appendix I, and as you gain in experience you will doubtless learn about them. But to start you off, the information below should be sufficient.

I wish to acknowledge my thanks to the companies listed here for making their products available to me for testing, and evaluation, and for other help they have given me in producing this book. I recommend their products, which I have used and tested thoroughly. Most of these manufacturers will gladly send you a catalog on receipt of a stamped, self-addressed envelope. They are arranged alphabetically.

Alfred Bernstein, 715–87th Avenue N.E., Minneapolis, Minnesota 55434. Manufactures custom-built sphere-making machines.

Duc-Kit Rock Hobby Accessories (The Ducketts), 32 Washington Street, Medford, Oregon 97501. Makes excellent diamond-saw kits, tumbler kits, drum-sander kits, polisher kits, and several other kit-form items of lapidary equipment.

The Foredom Electric Company, Route 6, Stony Hill, Bethel, Connecticut 06801. Foredom Flexible Shaft machines are almost a household word among toolmakers, craftsmen, and now lapidaries. They are excellent for carving minerals, as well as being useful in the making of settings and jewelry.

of precious minerals. The Ray-Tilt machine is a complete gem maker. They also make fluorescent equipment.

Shipley's Mineral House, Gem Village, Bayfield, Colorado, 81122. Besides supplying a gem drill and electric-wax pot for dopping stones, this company is a manufacturing jeweler, working in gold, silver, and platinum, both wholesale and retail.

Three-M Company, 3M Center, St. Paul, Minnesota, 55101. Makes diamond equipment. Marvelous diamond sanding belts are made by 3M as are precision faceting laps, and cupped diamond cabbing dishes. 3M also manufactures other diamond products useful in the lapidary shop, and will send information on its products to inquirers.

9.

Making Cabochons

It is estimated that there are nearly 6 million persons actively engaged in the cutting of gemstones in the United States, either commercially, as a hobby, or for the production of gems for jewelrymaking. The number of gem cutters increases by several thousand each year, and hundreds of companies are now flourishing in the manufacture of tools, equipment, and supplies for the lapidary art.

Many persons, including myself, were frightened away from cutting gems for years by the apparent intractability of the medium. Stone seems a completely unyielding and resistant material to work with, and, unfamiliar with the first principles of working gems, I assumed that cutting a gemstone would surely occupy my total waking hours for a long time, indeed.

When I visited a rock shop, whose owner was also a lapidary, and discussed the cutting of cabochons from his extensive stock of minerals. There were on display tray after tray of exquisitely polished stones of all sizes and shapes — his stock-in-trade, as it were. This pleasant and obliging man was more than willing to take time out to talk about his hobby and business, and he seemed justifiably proud of his ability to cut stones. Holding a chunk of rock in my hand, picked at random from one of his bins, I remarked that I wouldn't even bother to throw a rock like that at a dog!

With a smile the man opened a drawer and took out a slice of rock. "I have some of that material already sawed into slabs," he remarked. "Let me show you what it looks like when it's finished." Within minutes, holding the slab freehand, he had cut out a rough ellipse from it, having first marked the outline with a brass rod and a template. The cutting was done on a small diamond saw, running in a bath of oil to provide a coolant for the blade. Another minute or two and he had stuck the blank to the end of a piece of dowel with what looked to me like green sealing wax.

Maintaining a constant chatter about what he was doing, he led me to a grinder, where he commenced to shape the stone fastened to what I now know was a dopstick. Within a few minutes the piece of mineral took the shape of an elliptical cabochon, flat on the bottom, and smoothly rounded in all directions on the top.

The next stage was on another machine that had two drums covered with abrasive cloth belts. Explaining as he worked, he said, "The most important part of cutting is the sanding. The better you sand, the better polish you'll get." Turning the stone constantly, holding it against the wheel upon which he had water dripping, he smoothed out the ridges left by the grinding wheel. "Now you fine-sand it," he said, transferring his work to the second drum. "This is where you want to make sure you get every scratch out." Finally he stopped the drum, satisfied with the progress on the stone, and held the stick out for me to examine. I took it. The thing looked like a waterworn pebble. Gray, opaque surface, no marks showing on it at all. Rather like a piece of ground glass, except that it was dark in color. I was not impressed.

"Now let's polish it," the man said with a smile.

"How long is that going to take?" I asked, looking at my watch.

"Oh, two, three minutes. Maybe five." I looked at him in disbelief. He flipped the switch on another machine, this one having a disc covered with what looked like canvas. I later learned that that was just what it was—canvas. He sprinkled a little water on the fabric, then dusted a small amount of white powder on top. "Tin oxide," he confided over his shoulder. Holding the stone hard against the lap, he turned it every which way, making certain that he brought all parts of the surface into contact with the canvas. I could see that he was exerting considerable pressure on the stick. In a few minutes he examined the stone."O.K., that's good enough." He stopped the machine, swished the stone around in a can of water, then dried it with a soft cloth and again handed the stick to me.

I stood there looking at the stone and refused absolutely to believe what I saw. Surely he must have worked some sleight-of-hand, exchanging that ugly, dirty-looking chunk of rock for this beautiful treasure. Stuck to the end of the dopstick was a gem, a jewel, intensely black, streaked with a soft reddish-brown, and with a surface so brilliant that it looked liquid. I could easily see my own amazed reflection in the stone.

With a satisfied grin he took the stick out of my unresisting hands and said, "It isn't quite finished. I have to take it off the dop and fix the edges." He popped the stick into his soft-drink cooler and closed the lid. "Only takes a minute."

I was looking at the original chunk of rock that had started all these miraculous events. "Do you honestly mean to tell me that that jewel came out of a hunk like this?"

He nodded. Then he took the stick out of the cooler and pressed against the edge of the polished stone. It snapped off the sealing wax with a ping! Holding the stone in his fingers, he ran it against one of the sanding drums, beveling the sharp edge. Then, turning to me as he dried it again in the towel, he dropped it into my outstretched hand. "There you are, my friend. That's how cabs are cut." The entire operation had taken less than half an hour!

"Hold it up to the light," he directed.

When I did so, I could see that the gleaming black stone was in reality shades of black, gray, and brownish translucence. I could see through it, and the stuff looked like a liquid that had flowed around, mixing with the brown streaks.

"What is this?"

"Mahogany obsidian."

"May I buy this stone?" I asked.

"It's yours. Compliments of the shop."

I was hooked. I was also most unhappy. Much more than half of my adult life had just gone down the drain. I had thrown away all those years not cutting stones because I thought I couldn't live long enough to make them. Half an hour! In just half an hour I had been given a complete course in gem cutting. Complete enough to start me on the road to becoming a lapidary in my own right. All the essential operations had been performed before my eyes, and all I had to do was to put them into practice.

For many years I had been making jewelry of gold and silver, at one time commercially, more recently as a hobby for my family and friends. All those years I used gems purchased from various dealers around the country. What a waste! Not that the money spent for the gems was wasted—far from it; they are well worth their price. But what an immense satisfaction it is now to be able to say that a piece of jewelry that is the object of praise was made from scratch, from a "dog-throwing rock" and raw metal to the finished article. Of all the arts and crafts in which I have acquired some skill—more than twenty, in fact—gem cutting provides the most satisfaction, the greatest reward for the time spent. To take a chunk of rock that you would ordinarily kick out of your path as you walked across a field, and open it to discover a marvelously beautiful pattern of color and design inside, and then to make from a slice of that rock, a gem to be worn in a pendant, earring, ring, or other appointment, brings a joy not matched by any other endeavor.

It is in the hope that you can share this satisfaction that I now introduce you to the rewards of gem cutting, first of all with cabochons. Naturally, not all stones can be cut with the ease and short expenditure of time that my original piece of obsidian required. Some stones take a couple of hours to fashion, and much more time to sand to the point of polishing. Strangely enough, the polishing, which one would think as would take the longest time to perform, actually takes the least. Polishing is only a matter of a few minutes, even for very hard minerals.

CUTTING SLABS

The first step in cutting gems is the preparation of the cutting rough, as the material is called. Usually this rough is in the form of a piece of stone of almost any size and shape—that is, unless you are starting with a purchased slab. Many rock shops and mail-order houses sell cutting material in the form of slices sawed from the original rock. At every rock and mineral show where dealers have booths, such slabs are also sold. But, since the slab is part of step two in the art of gem cutting, we will disregard it here and assume that you are starting from scratch. You have a rock. Either you dug it up yourself or got it in a rock shop or show—the source is unimportant. And you must reduce this rock to slabs, or slices.

To slice minerals, you use a diamond saw. In years past, a *small* diamond saw blade cost several hundred dollars, and then it did not last too long. One forced cut on it and you threw it away. This in itself was enough to discourage most lapidaries from practicing the art. Much stone cutting was performed on what is called a "mud saw." This was a machine using a disc of steel as a blade, which ran with the lower part dipping into a slurry of abrasive powder and water or oil. The blade, picking up the abrasive, ran against the stone, wearing its way through the material being sawed. The stone was mounted in a carriage which traveled the length of the machine, keeping the rock pressed against the blade. The saw works, and in fact, many are still in use today, but it is slow—very slow—and the cuts are not nearly as true and smooth as those produced by the diamond saw.

Fortunately, we have relief from the fantastically high cost of diamond blades today. Methods of attaching diamond grains to the periphery of the blades have become routine, and the blades are now made in quantity in sintering ovens. A blade that once cost $200 may now be purchased for around $35, and the life of these modern blades is much longer than that of the old hand-charged ones.

The advent of man-made diamonds has further lessened the cost of blades, and the product is in no single way different from natural diamond powder. They are just as hard and cut just as fast, last just as long, and cost about one-tenth as much.

Diamond saws are made in many different sizes and styles. As outlined in the previous chapter, a well-equipped gem shop should have three, or possibly four. One uses a large blade. This is the slabbing saw. It is used to reduce the raw rock material to the slabs from which the gems themselves are taken. This saw should have as large a blade as your purse will allow, to permit your cutting large pieces of rock. (By the way, in this section of the book, I shall refer to the material we are working as "rock," for the most part, but please bear in mind that most of the chunks we will be working are actually minerals.)

You can buy your diamond saw complete, ready to plug in and run. They are very expensive, in the larger sizes. Or, if you are a combination machinist, welder, genius, and magician, you might build your own. The most practical way by far is to purchase a diamond-saw kit and assemble it yourself. In my own shop I use a 20-inch Duc-Kit diamond saw. This is an excellent machine, and has been in hard and constant use for over three years. The cost is about one-sixth the cost of a 20-inch saw already assembled, and the work it turns out is perfect. I have cut slices of agate and other minerals as thin as 1/32 inch with this 20-inch blade, without a single fracture or break. The slices are parallel and smooth—no blade ripples can be seen or felt on the slices.

Slicing

Rocks to be sliced must be fastened securely in the saw's vise. Usually the jaws of the vise are lined with wood or composition board, into which the rough surface of the rock digs to afford an even better grip. When mounting a rock in the saw, the carriage should first be run in as close to the saw blade as it can go. The

rock is now secured in the vise, projecting as far out as is safe. By this, I mean lock the rock into the vise with as little material between the jaws as you can with the rock still supported rigidly. As you tighten the vise, keep trying to move the rock with your hand. Only when you cannot budge the rock is it secure.

Now you may back off the carriage to make your first cut. I have a simple method that might work for you, too. In my Duc-Kit saw, four turns of the feed screw on the vise makes a slice about ¼ inch thick. Five turns produce a ⁵⁄₁₆-inch thick slab. After I have fastened my rock in the vise, I take up the slack on the crossfeed screw, then back off the carriage, counting the turns in groups of either four or five turns, depending upon

Opposite: *Slabbing a rock in the 20-inch Duc-Kit Diamond Saw.*

Below: *Small ends of minerals epoxy-glued to a block of wood can be sliced in the Lortone slab/trim saw down to the final end.*

whether I am slicing ¼-inch or ⁵/₁₆-inch slabs. Backing off, one, two, three, four; one, two, three, four; etc. I stop when the last bit of rock is presented to the saw to afford me a view of the pattern inside. In other words, the crust, or "heel," should be taken off in order for you to look at the cut surface to judge whether you wish to cut on that plane or not. Sometimes a piece should be cut in several different directions before you slice up the entire rock, because the pattern and even the colors sometimes change drastically from one angle to another, and there is really no way to tell just what the appearance of the slice will be until you have opened a "window" to look at it.

This means, of course, that you may have to go through the entire procedure of adjusting the carriage and mounting the stone in the vise several times. Just remember that you are working with material that took, perhaps, four hundred million years to form. It will take you a few hours to slice up. But it will take you only a few seconds to ruin if you don't take a little time at first to orient it in the best way possible.

Often a rock will show a very lovely pattern from one direction and an equally lovely, but entirely different, pattern from another direction. When this happens, many times I cut the rock halfway from one direction, taking as many slices as I can to the center, then re-orient the rock and finish cutting it in the other direction, thus getting slices of the same rock with different color distribution, pattern, and appearance. True, this method gives smaller slices on the second cutting plane, and can be employed only if the second direction of cutting will produce slices large enough for you to get the size cabochons you want out of them.

In my opinion, it is useless to cut slices thinner than ¼ inch. True, many rock shops sell slices as thin as ⅛ inch, but these cannot be used to produce good cabochons, because when you begin to grind, the curvature of the top is so flat that you cannot get good shape and polish on the surface. A cab, in order to show off the stone to its best advantage, should have a good rise to it. The larger the stone, the higher the rise must be. The shape should be a smooth and perfectly even curve from edge to edge, in all directions. Only practice will permit you to obtain this smooth and equal contour. It took me exactly three cabs to attain that skill. It should not take you much longer. If the slice from which you are cutting the cab is so thin that it does not permit you to cut the sides at a fairly steep angle before beginning to round over the top, then you will end up with a cab with a flat face, or one which has a flat center which you will find almost never takes a good polish.

So do not try to get the *most* number of slices from any given rock, but strive, rather, to get the *best* slices from it. Making a half-dozen excellent cabs from a stone by slicing it thick is far better than two dozen poor stones obtained by slicing it thin. The poor stones will have neither use nor beauty, and you just waste your material in attempting to get more slices. This caution is, I must tell you, valid only when you want to make cabs of some size. If you are making very small gems, then by all means take thinner slices, since the area regulates the height of a cab, and

Lace agate is an excellent example of a mineral that can be cut in several different directions to obtain different patterns.

stones of small area require lower profiles. A general rule to follow that might simplify your problem of how thick to saw is:

For oval cabochons 10×8mm and smaller, or rounds 7mm and smaller, you might slice ⅛ inch thick.
For oval cabs from 11×9mm to 14×12mm, or rounds from 8mm to 12 mm, cut the slices 3/16 inch thick.
Ovals from 16×12mm to 30×22mm and rounds from 14mm to 25mm in area should have slices not less than ¼ inch thick, and for stones larger than these sizes, cut a full 5/16-inch slice or even thicker, depending on just how large a stone you wish to make.

These rules are by no means fixed or set. They are merely a guide to help you judge how to work your material. You need not be bound by them, but you should bear them in mind if you buy slabs at shows or from rock shops, intending to cut certain-size stones.

My Duc-Kit saw has a screw feed for the carriage. The screw is driven by a three-speed pulley arrangement. The lowest speed moves the carriage a distance of 5/8 inch in five minutes; middle speed is 7/8 inch in five minutes, and the highest speed travels 1⅛ inches in five minutes. If the saw you use has adjustable carriage feed, you should use the lowest speed when you cut agates or minerals about the same hardness as agates, or quartz. The middle speed can be used for material such as obsidian, chrysocolla, sodalite, and similar substances. The high speed is used (by me) only for soft material like malachite, rhodochrosite, and the like. The difference in time between sawing at a low feed and a high feed is perhaps ten or fifteen minutes, depending on the size of the rock you are cutting. The life of the diamond blade is materially greater at lower speeds, and the blade will require sharpening less often.

It is a good practice, when sawing agate or other hard material, to sharpen your blade after cutting eight or ten slices of a medium size rock. Sharpening a diamond blade is simplicity itself. You merely saw a brick, or an old wornout grinding wheel, or, if you prefer, a couple slices off a saw-sharpening stone, such as those sold by Raytech. A diamond blade becomes dull when the steel on the edge melts and runs over on top of the diamond charge. The melting can be caused by several things, notably insufficient coolant when sawing rocks or too fast a feed for the hardness of the rock. On the other hand, some minerals glaze a saw blade no matter what feed or coolant you use. After you have run a diamond saw for a while you will become used to the "sing" of the blade as it cuts through rock. Any change in this "sing" should be immediately checked. As much as the cost of diamond blades has come down in the past couple of decades, they still cost a lot, and they should be closely watched to prolong their life.

There are several pointers in diamond sawing that you should become familiar with. First of all, if a saw is run under strain it can, and probably will, ruin the blade. Strain results if the rock slips in the vise, causing a binding of the blade in the cut; or if the blade is started against the rock on an angle, that is, the face of the rock applied to the beginning of the cut is at such an angle that the blade slips sideways as it enters the stone. A starting cut should be made as nearly perpendicular to the face of the rock as possible. Naturally, it is understood that this simply cannot be achieved with every rock, but when it cannot, the rock should be positioned in the vise to present as nearly a perpendicular face to the blade as possible. A small angle will not affect the entry cut. The feed is slow enough to permit the blade to cut a nick before it begins to slide on the stone. A nick is all that is needed to guide the blade true and evenly through the piece.

Forcing the feed of the carriage faster than the saw can cut the stone will result in one of two things. Either the blade will glaze, becoming dull and refusing to cut, in which case the rock will tend to ride up on the saw, pulling the carriage with it and finally jamming the blade, or the blade will glaze and begin to cut sideways, resulting in a curved cut, curving more and more until the blade walls are jammed between the sides of the cut in the rock. Then the blade will begin to heat up, finally becoming so hot as to warp, and the fun begins. Anything can go—the feed screw may strip its threads, the feed nut may strip out, or the saw blade may jam, stopping the motor, which may then burn out, while the carriage motor continues to run until it, too, jams and burns out.

All this is not intended to frighten you to the point where you are afraid to snap on the switch of your saw. On the contrary, if you are aware of the things that *can* happen, you can take care to see that they do *not* happen. Just follow the few simple rules. Be sure the material is securely clamped in the vise. Keep the saw blade sharp. Run at slow feed speeds, especially on hard material. Make certain you use enough coolant on the blade.

Coolants and Sumps

We now come to the subject of coolant. A diamond saw *must* be operated with an ample supply of coolant. Almost any liquid may be used. The trouble with water is that it rusts the metal parts of the machine. The trouble with kerosene is the smell, which some may find unpleasant. Ditto with diesel oil. There are additives which may be put into water to keep it from rusting machines using the mixture, and there are deodorants which may be added to kerosene to kill the smell. Personally, I use just plain old kerosene and I ignore the smell. It is cheap. It runs through a pump with no trouble at all. It washes the sludge down from the parts of the saw and keeps the blade clean. It does not stain 99% of the minerals cut. There are really no objectionable features about it, and I simply do not hang over the machine sniffing at it while it runs.

Coolant is applied to the blade of a diamond saw in any one of three ways. In the first, the blade dips into a sump of liquid as it revolves, carrying the coolant up and around as it runs. In the second, the coolant is dripped onto the top of the blade or onto the rock at the point of entry of the blade. In the third, the coolant is forcibly sprayed against both sides of the blade by a pump, which has a nozzle on each side of the blade below the cutting area. This is the method used in the Duc-Kit saw kits, and it is the best method so far in my opinion. It provides plenty of coolant — a surplus, in fact — which is infinitely better than an insufficiency. The surplus does not bother anything; it merely runs back into the sump.

My sump is a box made out of galvanized sheet iron, with two compartments separated by a wall 1 inch lower than the top of the partition. The kerosene runs out of the sawing chamber into the large part of the box and fills it up, finally overflowing into the small chamber through the holes in the partition. The pump is in the small chamber, and pumps the liquid back to the saw blade. As the saw operates, the rush of liquid all over the blade washes the sludge down with it into the sump. At intervals, the large chamber which acts as a settling tank is scooped out and the sludge discarded. A great amount of sawing can be done before the kerosene becomes so full of sludge that it has to be changed. With the enormous amount of sawing I do, I change the kerosene perhaps once or twice a year.

I have my sump mounted outside the sawing chamber on a shelf fastened between the legs of the saw, and before the saw is operated, the sump box must be filled with clean kerosene to the level of the holes in the partition. This ensures that the pump runs under the liquid — it will burn out if run in the open air — and the pumping action starts as soon as the saw is turned on. The liquid pumped out of the small chamber is soon returned as overflow from the large settling chamber and continues as long as the saw operates. When the cutting is completed, the kerosene drips off the machine, trickling down into the sump, filling it once more to the proper level. As a matter of fact, the level would slowly rise, due to the addition of sludge from the rocks being sawed, if it were not for the fact that the level also slowly drops due to the evaporation of the kerosene exposed to the air. The result is that the level remains constant for months at a time.

Pet stores and supermarkets sell cat litter for cat boxes to absorb the feces and keep down the odor. One brand, Cat Comfort, is an expanded clay substance, a clean, highly absorbent material that is of great value to the gem cutter. A box filled with Cat Comfort may be kept near the slab saw, and as the slabs are taken from the machine they can be buried for a moment in the Cat Comfort. All the kerosene is thereby pulled from the slab, and upon being removed from the box and wiped off with a paper towel, you will find the slab clean, dry, and ready for the next step. If your local pet store does not have Cat Comfort, or is unwilling to get it for you, a letter to the manufacturer, Georgia-Tennessee Mining and Chemical Company, Suite 810, 3379 Peachtree Road, N.E., Atlanta, Georgia 30326, will bring information as to where the material can be obtained.

TRIMMING THE SLAB

You now have your rock sliced into workable slabs, and are ready for the second step in producing a cabochon. You need two tools for this operation: a template for marking the stone and a trim saw for cutting it out of the slab. A large slabbing saw is entirely impractical for trimming and small work; for this work you must use a saw with a small blade, preferably around 8 inches in diameter and preferably mounted so the blade is on top of the work instead of behind or underneath. In this way you will be able to see exactly where you are cutting. H.O.P.E. manufactures the Preformer saw, which is an excellent overhead type.

Marking the Stone

There are several different kinds of templates on the market. All of them are good, but I prefer metal ones to plastic ones, simply because they wear longer and are a bit more rigid. The templates are made to fit standard setting sizes, and are marked in these sizes in millimeters. The stone is marked with a brass or aluminum scribe and a template. A short length of brass brazing rod, or a short aluminum knitting needle, makes an excellent marking scribe for minerals. The marks do not wipe off easily and will remain visible throughout the working of the stone. The scribe may be sharpened with a file, or on a grinding wheel.

Holding the slab in a good light, place the template on top, and, looking through the hole you have selected as the one you want to use, move the template around on the surface of the slab until you arrive at the portion that looks best to you. If the mineral you are working is transparent, it will help to hold both the slab and the template to the light as you move it, since you will then be able to see the design as it will look when the gem is finished.

Having selected the area that most appeals to you, hold the template tightly in position, and trace around the opening with the metal scribe. Put enough pressure on the scribe to make a

First position the template by moving it around on the slab to find the best part of the slab to use.

to permit insertion of the slab. The trouble with using a double template is that you cannot always get the opening you want to use over the area you want to mark out. The other solution is to take great care in grinding the edge of the stone, which will be discussed shortly.

Cutting Out the Shape

After tracing the shape, you now must cut it out of the slice on the trim saw. In using the Preformer, or any trim saw, the slab must be solidly held on the table. Make sure there are no chips of material under the slab, and make sure you hold the stone firmly while sawing. Do not try to force the blade through the stone, but

Trimming the blank on the H.O.P.E. Preformer Saw. Cut as close to the lines as possible and you will have less to grind later.

feel the way it cuts, then keep just enough pressure on the blade to permit it to cut its way through. If you have to make a long cut which necessitates your moving the slab, make certain you re-enter the blade exactly in the previous cut to avoid binding the blade. Let the blade feel its way into the cut before you put new pressure on it.

Trim as close to the line as practical. The more you take off on the trim saw, the less you have to grind off on the stone. Since a trim saw blade will outlast a great many stones, it follows that you should let the blade do the work, not the grinder. Make no attempt to trim off small areas so close to an edge that the blade will slide off before it has cut through the thickness of the slab. This will only dull the blade.

DOPPING THE STONE

After shaping, the blank stone is fastened to a dopstick for fur-ther working. A dopstick is a 6-inch length of dowel. Different-diameter dowels are used for different-sized stones. Use the larg-est dowel that is practical for the stone you are working. There should be space all around the stick for the dopping wax, without having the wax run over the edges of the stone.

Dopping wax is a hard type of sealing wax, specially blended for lapidary use. Usually it is dark green in color, and comes in sticks weighing about ¼ pound. The sticks are broken into small fragments, and melted in a dopping pot. There are several kinds of dopping pots available. I prefer the ones made out of a casting, since the thick metal in this kind of pot holds the heat much longer than sheet metal, and the wax re-mains soft longer. Whatever kind of melter you use, make sure that it is constructed so as to permit easy access to the melted wax and that it does not get so hot that it burns the wax.

The stone should be heated also. A cold stone will not adhere to the wax, and will fall off during some crucial period in the subsequent operations. The wax and the stone should both be hot enough to be quite uncomfortable when you touch them. Place the hot stone on a level surface with the side bearing the traced line up. Now, rotate a dopstick in the melted wax in order to coat the end of the stick for a distance of perhaps ½ inch, at the same time picking up a gob of wax on the end of the stick. Use a little discretion in the amount of wax you pick up. You need enough to make a good attachment to the stone, but not so much that it will run over the edges and cover the entire piece. A well-dopped stone will have the entire back face covered with wax and the wax carried up the dopstick to form a secure hold, but no wax at all over any edge of the stone.

Pick up a gob of hot wax on the end of the dopstick.

Shape the wax on the blank with the fingers, working rapidly so you do not burn yourself.

Now set the wax by dipping the dopstick in a can of cool water, unless you are working a heat-sensitive material, in which case you must air-cool it.

As you shape the wax to the blank, be sure to push it down firmly onto the stone to make good contact. The wax should stick to the mineral immediately on contact. If it does not, then the stone or the wax is not hot enough, and the operation should be redone.

As soon as the shaping of the wax is completed—and you should perform this operation as fast as you can to avoid having the wax set up as you work—the wax and the stone should be cooled to fix it in position on the dopstick. As you shape the wax, make certain that you keep the stick in the center of the stone and the stone squarely at right angles to the length of

Check to make sure the stone is perpendicular to the end of the dopstick before beginning to work it. If it is crooked, the wax must be rewarmed and the stone straightened.

the stick. It is most difficult to work a stone that is dopped crookedly.

To cool the piece, dip it into a dish of cool water, holding the dopstick upright so the stone will not sag out of square before the wax has had time to set up hard. This can happen, especially with a large and heavy stone. It takes only a minute or two for the wax to set and the stone to cool, at which time it may be removed from the water and dried off.

You may want to work several stones at the same time, in which case you cut out and grind them all, then dop them all in preparation for the next steps. It is an easy matter, especially if you are making a series of stones all the same size and shape, to get them all dopped up, and perform the same operation on them all, one at a time, taking them all through each step together instead of completing them one at a time. You get into a kind of routine in the work, which seems to make it go a lot easier and a lot quicker.

An assortment of blanks dopped up and ready to be ground into cabochons.

GRINDING THE STONE

Now you begin the actual shaping of the cabochon. Two different ways of grinding the face are used. For stones up to about 40×30mm, the wonderful diamond cabbing discs are decidedly better than any other method of grinding. These are made by the 3M Company and are supplied in grades from 100-mesh, 220-mesh, 45-micron, 30-micron, and 15-micron grits of diamond on 5-inch-diameter, slightly cup-shaped metal discs. These tools fit on a ½-inch mandrel and are operated with a water drip as a coolant and lubricant when working the stones. They should *never* be run dry.

If you intend making cabochons as a hobby—that is, more than just one or two once in a while—then a most useful piece of

This blanking machine was designed and built by the author. It will make any size and shape of cabochon blank automatically and in duplicate—as many as desired, one after the other. It employs one of the Tiara diamond wheels.

Shaping the outline of the blank is easy and accurate on a 3M diamond faceting disc. This one is mounted in a homemade machine.

The edge of the blank is first beveled to about 45 degrees. The Ray-Tilt Gem Maker is good for this purpose.

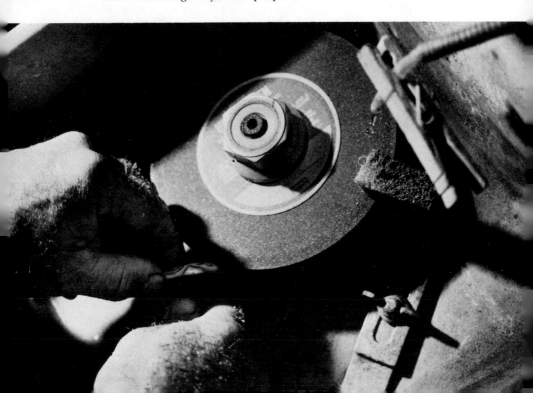

equipment is the Ray-Tilt Gem Making Machine. You may use a grinding stone on it or a diamond cabbing disc such as we have just discussed. Also, supplied with the Ray-Tilt are several interchangeable discs covered with sponge-rubber pads, on which are fastened the different grades and types of abrasive discs used in sanding and polishing. A water bottle and valve are supplied with the Ray-Tilt, eliminating the need for a constant water supply and making this machine ideal for use in trailer homes or in the field.

Assuming that the stone you are about to cut is not more than 40×30mm in size (larger stones will be discussed a little later on), the first step in grinding is to bevel the edges. The bevel is cut to approximately 45 degrees. The angle is not critical, but you should try to hold it as close to that as you can, because that angle is the easiest to work with in the subsequent steps of shaping. The edges are beveled until there is only a very thin edge left flat. This flat should not exceed 1/64 inch in thickness. It should just be wide enough to be easily seen with the eye as you work. If you have difficulty in holding such an edge, it might help you to mark around the edge of the stone with a pencil before you begin to bevel. The pencil line should be drawn right at the bottom edge of the stone, and the thickness of the line is just about right for the material left in place. Bevel right down to the pencil line, leaving the line in place.

One thing to learn and remember is that a stone being ground cuts much faster on a small, sharp curve than it does on a longer, shallower curve. If you are not aware of this tendency, you might cut the corners or sharp curved edges right off the stone, while the flatter sides of an oval, for example, yet remain to be ground down. The thing you wish to achieve is an even bevel all around the edge, with a very thin, flat edge remaining on the bottom of the blank.

Having achieved this goal, you now tilt the blank enough to grind a second bevel all around, removing about half of the first bevel, and making two steps on the edge of the stone in so doing. After this, make a third bevel, removing about half of the second, and so on, gradually rounding the stone from the edge to the center. You will reach a point where there is no more material to grind off as a bevel. At this point, examine the stone to see just how far you are from reaching the center of the top. You should still have a considerable flat area left on the face of the stone. This flat area must be ground to a smooth curve from all directions, and the curve must extend down the sides and edges to the narrow, flat edge left when the first bevel was made. Begin once again to bevel the edge, still leaving the original thin edge untouched. Grind a second bevel and a third, if necessary, making all these bevels a little flatter than you did the first time around. Grind the stone, keeping in mind the goal of achieving a smooth curve from the thin, flat edge to the center of the stone.

In gem shows, and in lapidary competitions, a cabochon is judged on several points. One of the most important is the symmetry of the curve from all angles. The next most important point is the symmetry of the shape and outline of the stone. In other words, the two most important things to keep in mind are to grind the shape of your stone accurately, and to grind the curved face accurately. A stone ground and polished with a lopsided shape, or an uneven curve on the face, is disqualified in competitions. Also, it looks very bad, and is ruined as a gem, even though the material it was made from is valuable and scarce.

Working from the edges inward, keep grinding to make the entire surface a smooth curve from edge to edge. There must be no flat remaining at the center, no matter how small, since the slightest flat will result in an uneven line or contour, and this flat, no matter how much time and care is spent in polishing the stone, will always show some scratches. They simply will not come out.

From time to time, hold the stone up about level with your eyes and examine the curvature. Grind as needed, to even out the curve. Always keep the stone moving against the grinding surface. Stopping even for an instant will produce a flat which will then have to be taken out by grinding the entire surface of the stone down to the lowest point of that flat.

Keep the center of the stone as high as possible. Grind the

The surface is now rough-ground to shape, using a 220 grit wheel.

The easiest way of grinding the rounded surface of a cabochon is with a 3M diamond cabbing disc on the Ray-Tilt machine.

Examine the surface frequently to ensure even grinding. The curve must be smooth and symmetrical from edge to edge, and no flats should be left on the top center.

center only enough to remove the flat area, shaping the curve down from the center to the edges. When the entire surface has been ground to a smooth, even curve, symmetrical in all directions, the stone is ready to sand.

SANDING THE STONE

Sanding is done on abrasive belts mounted on rubber drum wheels or on discs mounted on rubber-faced wheels in the Ray-Tilt machine. Faster work can be done on the drums, when using belts made by the 3M Company, which are covered with diamond powder. These are available in two grades: 220-mesh, and

15-micron for final sanding. Silicon carbide belts are also available in a wide variety of grades, from 100-mesh down to 600-mesh for final sanding.

I strongly recommend using diamond tools all the way through in gem cutting. The reason is that diamond abrasives cut smoother, faster, cleaner, and last from 50 to 100 times as long as any other abrasive material. The high initial cost is far outweighed by the life of the tool, and the ease and accuracy of cutting far exceed any other method.

The two grades of diamond belts are all you need to sand stones to the point where they can be polished. If you do not use the diamond belts, then you should use silicon-carbide belts in the grades 220 for the first sanding, 400 for the second sanding and 600 for the final sanding. You should have a machine for the

The final operation before polishing is to sand any remaining scratches out of the surface. The 3M diamond sanding belts on the Duc-Kit drum-sanding machine do a perfect job.

belts with at least two drums, to save the time and trouble of constantly changing the belt from one grade to another. Duc-Kit sells such a machine in kit form and also provides the expanding rubber drums for use with either diamond or silicon-carbide belts. They come in several sizes, the largest being 8-inch diameter drums, with the belts 3 inches in width. This is one of the standard sizes in which readymade belts are purchased.

Some small idea of the difference in life between silicon-carbide and diamond belts may give you an idea as to which type you want to use. A silicon-carbide belt will, with care and proper use, sand perhaps five or six medium-sized stones of a hard material like agate, before wearing out. This means, of course, that one belt of each of the three different grades mentioned above will sand a total of five or six stones, since all three belts are used in sanding each stone. A diamond belt, or rather a pair of diamond belts mounted on my Duc-Kit drum-belt machine, lasted me not quite two years, sanding a total of perhaps 350 to 400 stones. The diamond belts cost about $75 for a pair of 220 and 15 micron. Silicon-carbide belts cost about $1.25 each, regardless of the size grit on them, making a set of three come to about $3.75. One considerable difference in cost, yes, but now consider that you would have to use about 60 sets of silicon-carbide belts to equal the number of stones you can obtain from one set of diamond belts. You will have spent $225 for the silicon-carbide belts instead of the initial cost of $75 for the diamond belts. You will have had to change the belts 180 times during the making of the stones, instead of mounting them once and forgetting them. To my way of thinking, it simply doesn't pay to use other than diamond products. Even if you figure on a per-stone basis, the cost in sanding per stone comes to about 21¢ or 22¢ on diamond, as against 64¢ or 65¢ on silicon-carbide belts.

Drums to hold sanding belts are made in two different styles: expandable and expanding. These words are not synonymous in this case. The expandable drums have a split in the rim, and the drum is equipped with a lever which, when you are mounting the belt, tightens it on the drum by expanding the diameter of the drum enough to hold the belt in place. This works fine, except that there is a bump on each revolution of the belt, as the stone travels over the split. Expanding drums are covered with a very thick, endless belt of live rubber. The belt is pierced with many air gaps all around the circumference, leaving the smooth outer surface suspended on a row of many thin webs. The abrasive belt is slipped on over the drum and remains loose. It can be moved easily when the drum is stationary, but as soon as the machine is turned on, the drum expands from centrifugal force, tightening up the belt and running with a smooth surface.

The Duc-Kit machine is supplied with a hood to cover the drums and to protect you from splashing water, and with pet-cocks for regulating the amount of water fed to the drums. I like to work them with a generous supply of water, though my arms and shirt front get wet. You should never run the belts so dry that the stone leaves a whitish powdery streak. You *must* run the diamond belts with plenty of water, or you will shuck the diamonds right off the belts.

One important thing to remember when sanding on drums mounted under a hood is not to drop the outer end of the dop stick behind the hood front when you press the stone against the drum. This will cause the stick and the stone to jam in between the hood pan and the drum, tearing the belt off the drum and possibly cracking the stone, to say nothing of scaring you out of your wits as the whole machine rears up and roars at you. It is a mistake you will make only once; I speak from experience. Keep the outer end of the dopstick well up away from the front edge of the drip pan and hood assembly and you have nothing to worry about.

The stone is held against the belt with only enough pressure to cause the belt to cut. You will immediately feel the very slight pull of the belt when it is cutting. No more pressure should be applied, because the belt will not cut any faster, it will only wear out faster. This particularly applies to the diamond belts, since they cut so readily that much less pressure is required. At no time should the stone stop moving against the belt. Keep it rotating in a smooth, even curve, covering every point on the face of the stone. Over and over, touching each point, making sure

operation. Any slight inequalities — and I do mean *slight,* since a sanding belt removes practically no material — can be leveled on the belts.

The moment you apply the stone to the next-lower-grit belt, the surface which looked even and smooth to you before will now be simply covered with what look like gouge marks. The scratches put in by the 220-belt now appear enormous and deep by comparison with the scratches put in on the finer belt. You are now required to remove every scratch put in by the coarse belt, until the surface once more is covered with nothing but the scratches of the finer belt. In the case of the diamond belts, the surface will now be extremely smooth and have what is called a "prepolish" finish. It is ready to go to the polisher. In the case of silicon-carbide belts, the surface will now be covered with much finer scratches than those obtained with the 220-mesh belt. When the surface is once again smooth and even, the stone is sanded on the 600-mesh belt, exactly as before. Exactly as before, also, the stone will look gouged and dug up when you have applied it to the 600-belt for a time, and these old scratches must be taken off the surface to the last one.

When the sanding is finished, the surface of the stone, when dry, should have a slightly gray look, evenly dull in appearance, with perhaps just the suggestion of a shine to it. It will have a very slight shine if done on the 15-micron diamond belt. All of your long and tedious labor has now been completed, and you have only a few steps more to go before you can hold a glowing gemstone in your hands and feel the wonderful thrill of having produced it yourself.

POLISHING THE STONE

The next step is polishing the surface. In the instructions to follow, I am merely going to discuss the polishing lap. I am not going to go into the different surfaces used on the polishing laps,

Charging a leather-faced polishing lap in the Duc-Kit polishing machine. The stone itself is used to spread the moistened polishing compound.

Polishing the edge is tricky, and great care must be taken not to cut the polishing lap surface.

nor the different polishes and abrasives used for different stones., In the last section of this chapter you will find a table which, if followed, will tell you what surface and what abrasive to use for polishing many different kinds of minerals. It is a matter of course that you read this list *before* you begin to polish a stone, and pick out the combination of lap and polish to fit the stone you are working. The list is designed in such a way as to make the selection very easy—you merely look up the stone you are cutting and read off the required setup for polishing.

Polishing is done on a machine having a lap of one kind or another, using an abrasive of one kind or another, and wetted with water. The amount of water used is very little, and some gems polish better on a somewhat drier lap. Some need the lap quite wet. The action of a polish is to melt the surface of the stone, glazing it over until you achieve as nearly a liquid finish as possible. Some materials polish with great ease. Others take

Use both hands to steady the dopstick when polishing the stone. Tilt the stone to avoid catching the surface of the lap on the edges.

*Wipe the polishing compound from the surface and examine the stone
as you go. Every scratch should be sanded and polished out. The center
is the hardest spot to get clean and perfect.*

longer, and it is not the hardness of the material that determines
the ease of polishing, but rather the amount of heat and pressure
it takes to melt the point of contact.

I can now explain what I meant when I stated that a flat left
in the top of a stone, no matter how small, simply would not
come out or polish. When you apply the surface of a curved
stone against the polishing lap, the point of contact is actually
just that — a *point* of contact. It is a simple matter of physics that
the energy it takes to heat up a tiny point is far less than the
energy required to heat up a large flat area. In the case of polishing the surface of a stone, the amount of energy required to
polish a curved surface is not greater than that which you can
supply with your hands and arms, meaning that even a child can
polish a stone. But if you attempt to polish a flat stone, you will
work like a horse and never achieve the same liquid surface sim-

ply because you are not strong enough to apply sufficient pressure to heat up the entire surface. Flats, slices, large pieces such as the faces of book ends, ash trays, and similar things must be polished on a different machine and with a different technique. We will go into that later on. Gemstones must have curved surfaces to achieve a high polish in a short time.

The first rule you must follow in polishing your gem is to hold it firmly by the dopstick, supporting the stone with your fingertips if it is a large one. Above all, take great care that the edge of the stone is never presented to the polishing lap in such a way as to catch the lap. One of several things will happen if you do so. First, the lap will snatch the stone out of your hands and slam it against the guard, possibly cracking it in the process. Next, the stone can rip the surface off the lap, completely ruining it for further work. There is also the possibility of the dopstick catching between your fingers when the lap is trying to snatch it away from you, resulting in a severe strain if nothing worse.

Always present the surface of the stone to the lap in such a manner as to permit the lap to run off the edge, never onto the edge. If the lap is rotating counterclockwise, for example, and you are polishing on the edge of the lap nearest to you, the lap will be rotating from your left to your right hand. The stone should always be held with a slight tip to your right, so the lap is running under the face of the stone and off the edge in contact with the lap. In order to polish all the edges of a stone, the stone must be rotated as it is held against the lap. A considerable pressure is needed to hold the stone down. On the other hand, you do not want to exert so much pressure that you stall the lap. You will very shortly be able to tell the best amount of pressure for the stone you are working.

While there is no set rule to follow in the order of which part of the gem to polish first, it is my habit to polish first all the edges, down to that fine, flat edge which you now have sanded into a thin, flat bevel, and which you do not have to polish at all. I run the stone upended on the lap until the entire edge has been polished, and then slowly turn the face down to polish the surface. At the final step, hold the dopstick in both hands to keep it steady, while you press it straight or very nearly straight down to polish the center of the stone.

After perhaps five minutes of polishing, after you have made certain that the entire surface and all edges have had a good rubbing against the lap, wipe the stone off and examine it. It should be finished, and you should catch your breath in amazement at the brilliance and beauty of the thing you have created. If there are any dull spots remaining, apply pressure again on the polishing lap until these are removed. Just a swipe or two should suffice.

However, if any scratches are visible, that means you did not sand the stone enough before you started to polish, and you must go back again to the drums and do the sanding job over again. First, examine any scratches on the polished surface. If they are very deep, it means they were left over from the first grinding, or the 220-belt, and you will have to go on down through the intermediate stages in order to remove them. If the scratches are moderately fine, they probably have been left from the 440-belt, and you can start again with that stage. Extremely fine scratches can be removed by sanding again with the 600-belt or the 15-micron diamond.

This time, you need only sand the scratched area, not the entire surface of the stone. Sand them enough to remove the scratches when viewed under a magnifying glass with the surface of the stone dried completely. Fair the sanding out around the scratched area so as not to leave a flat sanded into the surface, then again polish the stone on the lap. You may have to repeat these operations a couple of times before you get all the scratches out, but you will quickly learn how to sand enough so as to eliminate most of the repeat work.

Do not be satisfied with anything but a perfect job of grinding, sanding, and polishing. Remember that you are working with a piece of material that is absolutely unique. In the entire world, in all the billions of billions of tons of that particular mineral there may be in the crust of this planet, you will never find another piece that is the exact duplicate of the one you hold in your hand, glued to the end of a piece of dowel. Such individuality deserves the very best job you can possibly do on it. If you have to repeat an operation a dozen times to make it come out right, by all means do so. The end result will be worth the effort and time.

FINAL STEPS

After the polishing is completed, the stone must be removed from the dopstick. No, you do not have to lay it on an anvil and beat it with a sledge hammer to make it come loose from the wax. I grant that the tenacity with which the stone clung to the wax all through the thumping, scraping, and rubbing of the various operations you just put it through might make you believe that it was on the end of that stick to stay, but such is not the fact. Simply jam the stone down in a bowl or pan of icecubes, or lay it inside your home freezer for five or ten minutes. Then

Place the polished stone on the dop in the freezer for a few minutes, then the stone will pop right off the wax when pressure is applied to an edge with the fingers.

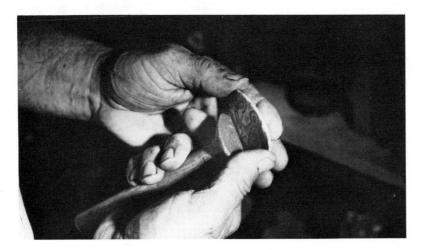

remove it, apply pressure with the end of your thumb or finger to the edge of the stone, and *ping!* — it will snap off the wax easily and cleanly. It will snap off so suddenly that you can snap it across the room if you are not expecting it, so take care to snap in such a way that you can catch the stone as it comes free. Any tiny chips of wax remaining on the back of the stone can now be scraped off with the blade of a pocket knife while the stone is still cold.

Only one more operation remains.

On the coarse belt of the sanding machine, you must now break all the sharp edges on the bottom of the stone. Holding the gem in your fingers, touch it to the belt, with the bottom of the stone up, and sand very lightly, rotating the stone so all the edge is brought into contact with the belt. Just the sharp knifelike edge is taken away in an extremely small bevel. This operation serves two purposes. When the stone is set, it will slip into the bezel

After removing the polished gem from the dopstick, break the bottom edges slightly on the drum sander until a slight even bevel shows all around.

much more easily if the bottom edge is beveled. But even more important, the bevel on the bottom edge keeps that edge from chipping, as it easily would if it were not beveled.

Your gem is now complete. You have created a thing of beauty from a very ordinary-looking piece of the planet on which you live. Treat it with reverence and lots of T.L.C. and it will continue to give you joy throughout your life, and also your descendants, because a gemstone, properly cared for, will remain beautiful for centuries. It is the most *permanent* object of beauty you can conceive, and only in very rare instances, in very rare minerals, will the wondrous polish and luster and color ever fade or become dull.

MATERIALS USED FOR POLISHING

As stated above, different minerals require different materials for polishing. Some require one kind of abrasive, and others a particular type of powder.

The polishing compound most universally used is tin oxide. This material will polish a great number of minerals, and it is the only compound that can be used for some stones. Tin oxide comes in the form of a white powder, slightly sticky, and is used in small quantities on the polishing lap. For that matter, all the compounds are used sparingly, and you will find that the gemstone polishes far better and much faster than if the lap is loaded with polishing medium.

Cerium oxide is perhaps second in popularity as a polishing material. This is a tan powder, of about the same consistency as tin oxide, but lighter in weight.

Chrome oxide is also a very useful polishing compound, but it has the great disadvantage of coloring everything bright green, including the polisher! It is difficult to wash off your skin.

Iron oxide is another good polishing material, but this one is even better at staining than chrome oxide. In the case of iron oxide, everything is bright red when you get through.

An excellent polishing medium is Linde A. I find that the material sold by Raytech under the name "Raybrite A" is exactly the same in action as Linde A and about one-third the cost. Either of these powders will do the job when all else fails.

The materials of which polishing laps are made vary as much as the polishes themselves. The commonest lap covering is canvas. The heavier the better, and if the cover is made with a drawstring around the edge it will eliminate the troublesome chore of folding the material around the lap head and tacking it in place.

Leather is also an excellent polishing-lap cover. It can be used either with the flesh side or the hair side out. It has disadvantages both ways. The disc of leather should be cemented to the lap with a removable type of cement sold for the purpose by lapidary supply companies. This way the leather can be renewed when it finally wears out.

The third lap material is felt. This is usually employed in the form of hard felt wheels, or thinner hard felt discs fastened to the polishing head with removable cement. When using felt as a polishing surface you must be very careful not to overheat the stone, since felt generates more heat than do the other materials used for this purpose.

Several other substances have been used for polishing heads with various amounts of success. Pellon cloth is one of these, and short-napped, rubber-backed carpet tiles are another. Soft wood, fiberboard, Masonite, and many other materials all have some use, but if you stick to canvas, leather, and felt polishing lap, you will be able to do everything needed in creating gemstones.

The heads of the polishing machine are usually made of flakeboard or plywood. These should have a pad of resilient material placed under the final covering. A disc cut from one of the carpet tiles is excellent for the padding, and it can be placed on the head loose, without cementing in place, if the covering is drawn around the edges of the lap and secured in some way. The use of such a pad makes the polishing easier and faster, since when pressure is placed on the stone the rubber gives, permitting the fabric of the cover to run up on the sides of the stone, and also to rub over a rounded top surface without missing any spots. When polishing on a hard surface, there is the possibility of a slight flat on the stone being skipped over and not polished. Of course, you have been warned that there should be no flats on the surface of a cabochon, so you should never be troubled with this difficulty. The kit supplied by Duc-Kit comes equipped with drawstring canvas covers and rubber pads for the heads.

As a general rule, hard stones can best be polished with the rubber backing under the polishing material, and stones with hard and soft areas polished best on hard surfaces, such as leather, or Pellon cloth on the lap without rubber backing. This will eliminate undercutting as much as possible, the hard lap riding over the softer areas without cutting any of the material away. Also, on minerals which you find to undercut, be very sparing of the polishing compound, since too much of that will pack up in the soft areas and pull material right out, with the same result as though you had used a soft backing pad.

Some massive material is polished with very dilute hydrochloric acid in the compound. About ten drops of 5% acid added to an ounce of water, and this mixed with the polish, will help achieve a good polish on otherwise intractable materials such as azurite, malachite, and many other carbonates, especially the copper carbonates.

Naturally, the use of acid in the water requires extra care; you don't want it on your skin or clothes. Also, the acid will rapidly deteriorate the material of the lap covering, so you would not want to use this method for just one stone. Rather, you should wait until you have a good number of gems to polish, then do them all at the same time. Then the deterioration of the fabric covering of your polishing lap will not be so painful.

The plastic Ultralap discs from Pfizer Company are convenient for many types of polishing. They are made in tin oxide, cerium oxide, and chrome oxide, as well as in the finer grades of silicon carbide for sanding. In ordinary use they are cemented to the rubber backing pad mounted on a disc to use in the Raytilt Gem Making Machine, as well as on other gem makers.

I shall list a few of the more popular minerals for gem cutting in this chapter, together with the methods I prefer for polishing. Please realize that these are merely the methods I use in my own lapidary shop. In your shop other methods and materials may prove far easier and bring just as good results.

azurite   Polish in two stages. First, with Raybrite A on slightly dampened leather without rubber backing pad. Finally, polish on soft felt with chrome oxide, rather wet, and with very gentle pressure and slow speed. To achieve slower speeds on a single-speed lap, polish closer to the center of the head, where the surface speed is considerably diminished.

beryl   The best polish is obtained on leather with Raybrite A. Cerium oxide on hard felt will also produce a brilliant polish.

calcite   Use tin oxide on canvas for best results. Most calcite cut for gem work is in the form of onyx, and this mineral will take a better polish if a very small quantity of powdered oxalic acid is dissolved in the water when mixing the polishing medium.

chrysoberyl   In the cabochon form as cat's eyes, polish on leather with Raybrite A, or with 6000- to 8000-mesh diamond spray on felt. Sometimes a wooden lap will give better results than leather. Use almost dry.

copper rhyolite   This material polishes very easily on a leather lap using Raybrite or Linde A.

corundum   For polishing this very hard and tough material you must use a lap made of copper. Grinding is also done on copper laps, with diamond powders replacing silicon-carbide powders. If only a stone or two is being produced, a wood or leather lap can be used and the stone polished in two stages. First stage should be with 1200 diamond powder or spray, and the final polish with 6000 to 8000 diamond.

epidote   The massive material used for cabochons may be polished on canvas laps using tin oxide, or on felt using cerium oxide.

garnet   Raybrite A or Linde A on leather laps are used for the various species of garnets. Chrome oxide can also be used on leather. Almost dry seems to give the best results.

hematite   This red oxide of iron appears black in the stone and takes a polish so bright as to appear as a mirror. Use cerium oxide on canvas, fairly damp.

howlite   Tin oxide on felt or on canvas will impart a good polish to this mineral. It tends to undercut quite badly, so apply minimal pressure. If it still undercuts too much, try the same polishing compound on leather without a rubber backing pad.

jadeite   Use a leather lap and Raybrite A for this tough mineral. It also undercuts, so watch the progress very carefully. The lap should be nearly dry.

jet   Polishes well on canvas with tin oxide. This is a very soft material and care must be taken when working it.

labradorite   A feldspar mineral. This polishes very well on felt with cerium oxide. Use fairly dry, and stop polishing at frequent intervals to permit the stone to cool.

lapis lazuli   Chrome oxide on a leather lap for this lovely mineral. Linde or Raybrite A can also be used.

lazulite   Chrome oxide on leather polishes this mineral easily. If you do not want to endure the mess this intense green material makes, use Raybrite A or Linde A.

lepidolite   This mineral undercuts so readily that great care must be taken when polishing. Perhaps the best method is to use a wood or hard leather lap with cerium oxide. The cerium-oxide Ultralap discs will work well, especially if they have the rubber backing pad removed and are used on the hard surface of the disc.

malachite This is one of the minerals mentioned earlier as being improved by the use of dilute acid in polishing. Chrome oxide on leather for the first polish, then a second polishing by hand with a chamois and solution of chrome oxide, with a little dilute hydrochloric acid added, will produce a brilliant polish. Wash everything well after using the acid solution.

marcasite Linde or Raybrite A on leather is good for this sensitive mineral. It should be very slowly heated when dopping to avoid fracturing. Do not chill in water to set the dopping wax.

microcline Polishes well on felt with cerium oxide. This is another of the feldspar minerals.

moonstone Same as the above mineral. This is a feldspar, too, and will take a good polish on felt using cerium oxide as the polishing medium.

nephrite This mineral, together with jadeite, is classed as jade and is worked the same as jadeite. Raybrite A on leather is best for this tough material. Also, chrome oxide on leather or tin oxide on wood can be used successfully.

obsidian This wonderful volcanic glass takes a mirror polish using tin oxide on canvas or cerium oxide on felt. It is very brittle, and you can very easily snap a stone in two if excessive pressure is brought to bear on the polishing lap. Also, a stone may fracture on the dopstick if it gets too hot, so polish with several stops to permit the stone to cool.

opal Be careful when polishing this stone not to permit it to overheat. Use cerium oxide on felt, and keep the polishing lap quite damp to wet.

peridot Raybrite A, Linde A, or chrome oxide on leather will polish this mineral with difficulty. It is a hard, slow process. A few drops of acid added may help.

prehnite Chrome oxide on leather will polish prehnite easily. Watch for undercutting at times, and regulate your polishing pressure to suit the stone. Use the lap nearly dry.

psilomelane Sometimes called black malachite. This mineral undercuts in bands if you are not careful. It polishes on leather with Raybrite A or chrome oxide, but the chrome oxide tends to stain the soft areas between the bands of harder material.

pyrite Raybrite A on leather will polish pyrite easily. It is very sensitive to heat, so care must be exercised in dopping and polishing not to overheat the stone.

quartz A great number of gem minerals are quartz in one form or another, and the treatment of them all is so similar that one listing is all that is necessary. However, since many beginning rockhounds do not know all the different varieties of this ubiquitous mineral, I shall first enumerate a few of the more popular kinds. Among the quartz minerals used for gem cutting are: agate, jasper, prase, aventurine, tigereye, smoky quartz, rose quartz, onyx, sardonyx, amethyst, carnelian, chrysoprase, and petrified wood. There are many more, but this will give you an idea of the different mineral names in the quartz family. Perhaps the best polish is obtained on felt with cerium oxide, but I have also had excellent results using tin oxide on canvas and Raybrite A on leather, only slightly damp. Rose quartz, cat's-eye, and tigereye are three of the quartz minerals that often show asteriation. This type must, of course, be oriented properly to display the star in its strongest aspect. Tigereye undercuts very badly, and best results are obtained with this touchy mineral on leather with Raybrite A or Linde A.

rhodochrosite This very beautiful and somewhat costly material is difficult to work because of its weakness of structure. Sharp corners must be avoided or they will be almost certain to break off during polishing, grinding, or setting in jewelry. The material also undercuts, due to the hard and soft bands. Leather laps charged with Raybrite A or tin oxide give the best polish. Wood laps are also good, and these should be dampened a bit more than the leather lap.

rhodonite   This is also a pink-to-red mineral, but rhodonite often is shot through with black areas, making a delightful contrast of color in the finished gem. Massive and granular, it must be treated gently to avoid fracturing and undercutting. About the only way to obtain a good polish is to use a leather lap with Raybrite A or Linde A.

serpentine   This very soft mineral is known by many names — verde antique, williamsite, bowenite are just a few. To polish, use a leather lap nearly dry, and chrome oxide as the polishing compound.

shattuckite   Little known, but a very beautiful gem mineral when obtained with only a few inclusions of base minerals. It undercuts so badly when these are present that it is disheartening to try for a perfect polish. Try it on the Pfizer Ultralap discs coated with tin oxide. Raybrite A and Linde A on leather will also give good results, but the leather should not be backed with rubber, or the surface will give too much when the stone is in contact.

sodalite   This vibrant blue mineral polishes to a liquid surface on felt using cerium oxide. A softer polish, not nearly so brilliant, is obtained with tin oxide on canvas. The Ultralap discs of cerium oxide also work very well with small stones.

spodumene   Known under two names: when green or blue it is called *hiddenite* and when pink or violet the name is *kunzite*. Sometimes found in fibrous masses which make "cat's-eye" gemstones. Polish them on leather with Raybrite A.

thomsonite   This valuable mineral must be polished with care because it is full of hard and soft spots which will make the gem turn out lopsided if you are not careful. The soft parts are very soft and cut away readily. Best to doublet each nodule before beginning to grind and polish them. Cerium oxide on felt gives the best polish.

topaz   Polish this mineral on a leather lap with Raybrite or Linde A.

tourmaline   A leather lap charged with chrome oxide will polish tourmaline nicely. Some of this mineral is porous, and the pores must be sealed by heating the stone and dipping it in melted wax for a minute or two, then wiping it off and polishing it. The wax may be removed later by soaking in benzene.

turquoise   Raybrite or Linde A on leather or on canvas will produce a good polish on turquoise. Soft and fragile, so take care not to break the stone while polishing.

variscite   This mineral is by way of becoming extinct, due to overmining the limited sources. Good variscite is very costly, but worth every cent of its price. It looks somewhat like turquoise, and handles much the same. It will polish very easily on a leather lap with Raybrite A, on a canvas lap with tin oxide, or on a felt lap with cerium oxide. A felt lap may also be used with tin oxide, if you prefer.

10.

Cutting Opals
and Other Precious Stones

Opals are almost like narcotics. Once you have been subjected to the amazing beauty of this precious mineral, you are hopelessly addicted. Unfortunately, opals are not cheap. Some of them are more costly than diamonds, and deservedly so. I know of no gemstone with as much color, fire, and just plain beauty as an opal.

The finest opal in the world is found in the United States at Virgin Valley, Nevada. The trouble is that this material fractures so easily and so completely on being removed from the ground that it is useless for gemstones. Only as a lump for a museum specimen is the Virgin Valley opal collectible. For this reason, opal from Australia became known as the finest opal to be found. The opals from "down under" are truly magnificent gems and deserve every bit of their fantastic reputation. Different kinds of opals come from different areas of that country, and two of the most famous diggings are Coober Pedy and Lightning Ridge. Andamooka opals are wonderful for their flashing colors.

The Queensland Opal Cutters, Box 734, Surfers Paradise 4217, Queensland, Australia, has for some time offered a course in opal cutting at a very reasonable price. The course includes a good quantity of cutting material and at least one piece of good-

174

quality rough opal from which a sizable gemstone can be obtained. With the cutting material is a book giving directions on how to handle opal and how to produce gemstones from it. I am indebted to the Queensland Opal Cutters for one of these courses made use of in this chapter, and directions I give here are essentially the same as those recommended by this reputable firm. I followed their instructions faithfully, then made a few changes in techniques to accommodate the tools and equipment available here.

To begin with, precious opal is just that — precious. Really good cutting material is very costly and very difficult to obtain. For this reason, great care must be taken not to waste any more than is absolutely necessary to produce your gems. For sawing the pieces into individual slices, a thin-kerf saw is a necessity. You can actually lose material worth the price of the complete diamond-saw machine in one cut off a piece of rare opal if you use a thick-kerf or standard saw blade. So it certainly pays to invest in a thin-kerf saw if you intend to work with opal, beryl, ruby, or any other of the more costly gem materials. The thin-kerf Raytech Diamond Saw is an excellent machine for handling these minerals. The blades remove only about 12/1000 inch of kerf, which is about as thin a cut as one can produce.

Besides being costly, opal is fragile. It is heat-sensitive to a degree, and great care should be taken when dopping the pieces for grinding and polishing. In fact, great care should be taken with every step of the operation in cutting opals. This is one material where the processing steps cannot be hurried.

Opal occurs in many varieties, only four of which will be discussed here. *White opal,* sometimes called *Queensland opal,* is milky white with flakes of color through it. If the flakes are very large, the material is called *harlequin opal. Black opal* is of gray-to-black base with a play of colors in the form of patches or flakes within the material. Black opal, to my mind, is the most dramatic of all opals. The black opal with large areas of intense reds, blues, greens, and oranges is sometimes called *black fire opal,* and this material is one of the most costly of all opals. Fire opal has a transparent to translucent reddish to orange base with a play of color internally. *Jelly opal* comes from Mexico and is transparent to translucent, almost water clear, with a wonderful play of soft colors inside the stone.

Except in very rare cases, opal is cut as a cabochon gem. In the case of thin-seam sections of the black variety, they are made into doublets with a flat or very nearly flat face, backed with quartz, opal potch, obsidian, or agate. Potch is a poor grade of opal, and is used extensively as doublet backing because it has the same coefficient of expansion as the precious material and is not likely to set up strains in the gem during temperature changes. Agate or quartz is just as good, because—and many people are unaware of this fact—opal *is* quartz. The chemical formula of quartz is SiO_2 and that of opal is $SiO_2.nH_2O$, which is merely quartz with an indeterminate amount of water in its composition. Opal is softer than plain quartz, having a hardness of 5.0 to 6.0, as against 7.0 for quartz.

This softness is another reason why care must be taken in working opal, and why opals should be set in jewelry in such a manner as to protect the surface as much as possible from wear and contact with hard surfaces. When used as a ring stone, an opal should never be worn constantly. When you wish to display an opal ring, wear it for the function at hand, always remaining conscious of the fact that you must protect the gem from impact or rubbing against hard materials. Then, after the function is over, remove the ring and store it safely in your jewelry box.

This might seem like a lot of trouble, and perhaps it is, but if you want to enjoy the enormous beauty of this rare and valuable gem material, then you should be prepared to go to the trouble needed to preserve that beauty and value. Opals set in pendants are not subjected to the same hazards of wear as are stones set in finger rings. Earrings are also a practical way of wearing opals.

Selecting Rough Opal

The selection of the rough when working with opal is most important. When you order opal, a dealer is not going to pick over his stock to select the very best pieces he has to fill your needs.

He will more than likely pick up the first piece closest to your requested size and send it to you. Often dealers will send a package of several pieces of rough on approval. The opal is priced in several different ways. A figure may be put on the entire package, in which case you must take it all. Or each piece may be priced separately, which permits you to pick out the piece you prefer, or, in some cases, the dealer will state that the package may be upgraded—that is, you may pick out the best pieces and return the rest. Usually, when this is the case, the dealer "loads" the price of the rough—say, 10% over the quoted price. This covers his losses on the poorer-quality rough left after the best pieces have been taken from the lot. This also means that you pay 10% more for the rough, but, in view of the fact that you are able to cull out the lesser quality pieces, this additional cost does not seem too much. Bear in mind that precious opal is expensive to begin with, and whether you pay $50 or $55 for a piece does not make that much difference.

The finest grades of Australian black opal sell for from $500 to $1500 per ounce. The cheapest types of opal sell for as little as $2 per ounce. The quality of the material establishes the price, or rather, the price is increased according to the color and quality of the material. Needless to say, $2 opal is not worth very much, even when carefully cut and polished.

It is far better to buy opal rough over the counter instead of through the mail, because then you can examine each specimen closely before committing yourself to purchase it. Any reputable dealer will let you examine any piece he has for sale as much as you want to. He will provide you with a good light under which you may turn the piece around, searching out the best color flash areas, and determining if it will suit the idea you have for cutting a gem from it. Avoid buying opal which is shown to you in a pan or jar of water. Water will hide fine cracks which appear only when the piece is dry. Any liquid will act as a cover for hairline fractures. It is best to look at rough in the dry state.

Opal usually occurs in seams and veins in the matrix rock, sometimes so thin that the precious material shows only as a line across one face of a lump of rock. You must determine if the

rough is thick enough to permit cutting of the stone you want
from it, since the finest color flash is seen when the rough is
viewed edge-on. Sometimes, as in the case of most black opal,
the line of color is so thin that a stone cannot be cut across it at
all. Usually, this variety of opal is made into doublets, a technique that will be discussed later on in this chapter.

In any event, when selecting your piece of rough, try to
imagine the stone you want to make, resting inside the piece you
are examining. Visualize, if you can, the size and shape of the intended jewel *within* all surface flaws and blemishes. You must
take into consideration the level of the deepest hollow on the
surface of the rough, and plan your gem below this level. This
visualization must be done with the areas of color taken into
consideration as well as the surface shape. It would do no good
to plan a stone around the shape of the rough, only to find that it
was oriented in such a way as to kill all the fire and play of color
resting in that piece of mineral.

Perhaps your first attempts to plan a stone in this way will
not have optimum results. It is possible that the dealer from
whom you are purchasing the rough can help you, if you tell him
what you want. You can learn only from experience, and sometimes gaining that experience is rather painful. However, by
using good judgment and exercising care in working the piece,
you are sure to end up with a gem of beauty, even if it is not exactly what you had intended to make in the first place.

You should never, in the case of precious gems, at least, try
to cut a stone to fit a particular setting, unless you are actually
replacing a stone which has been broken out of a setting; under
such circumstances you are forced, naturally, into cutting a stone
for a particular place in an item of jewelry. The cutting of precious stones should be governed by the size, shape, and color
distribution of the rough material. Not all gems can be cut from
an even slice of cutting material. Sometimes the piece of rough is
just large enough to take one good gem from it by careful trimming away of any waste and potch. Only after the gem has been
cut to the maximum size and shape possible from the piece are
you ready to give thought to the setting into which it will fit. The
setting is then made to fit the gem, not the reverse.

Cutting an Opal

Once you have planned the gemstone, the excess material must be trimmed away on the thin-kerf saw. The piece is trimmed as close to the rough blank of the gem as possible, taking into consideration any natural shaping of the rough to save trimming work. All the chips and small pieces of precious opal should be carefully retrieved and put away for future use. They will make interesting "floating gems"—small glass spheres filled with opal chips and glycerin—if they are too small for anything else.

Opal must be cut slowly and with plenty of coolant because of its heat sensitivity. At no time should the temperature of the material be brought up to the point of discomfort to the fingers. Nearly any coolant is good to use with opal, but the mineral should not be left standing in oil coolants for days on end. As a matter of fact, it should not be left in a machine longer than it takes to perform the work necessary to trim or shape it.

Grinding an Opal

After the excess is trimmed away, the base should be ground flat. This is done best on one of the 3M diamond-faceting discs. A fine disc will serve best, because no further finishing will be needed on the base. Always bear in mind the possibility of a change of plan when roughing out an opal. The part you cut away may reveal hidden beauty far greater than that which was visible in the rough, so that the surface you are lapping flat for the base may very well turn out so much more dramatic and colorful that it will be used as the top instead. For this reason—the revealing of hidden color—opal should be cut or ground very little at a time, with frequent stops for examination. Always dry the stone to examine it and to make certain you are not exposing a hidden crack or flaw. Then the stone may be wetted to reveal the play of color before you return to the grinding.

The next step after lapping the base is to fasten the stone to the dopstick for grinding the top. This is done the same way as with any other stone, but more care must be taken not to raise the temperature too high. The piece of opal should be placed on the heater with an insulator under it. This insulator may be a piece of asbestos paper, hard asbestos sheet, or even a small piece of cardboard. The platform of the dopping-wax melter should get as hot as the melting pot holding the wax. A small chip of dopping wax is placed on top of the piece of opal and the pot watched carefully. As soon as the wax on the stone begins to melt, the stone is hot enough and should be dopped immediately. Never quench a dopped opal in water. The sudden chilling will fracture the stone just as easily as overheating. Position the dop so the stone will not drift in the soft wax and permit it to cool in the air until the wax has set. After all the latent heat has left both the wax and the stone, you may dip it in cool water to harden the wax still further if you wish.

After the dop is cooled and ready to work, you should make an attempt to pick the stone off the dopstick. It is far better to find it loose and have to dop it a second time than have the stone pop off a dop in the middle of an operation, slamming against the side of the machine with possible damage or even fracture as the result. If the stone is tight on the wax, it is now ready for grinding.

The same precaution against overheating while dopping must be taken when grinding the stone to shape. An abundance of coolant must be on the stone at all times, and you should stop grinding frequently and press the stone against your cheek to feel the temperature. If it begins to feel warm at any time, stop work until the material has cooled. Then once again you may apply it to the grinder. Do not use coarse wheels when grinding opal, since they transmit greater shocks to the gem than do the fine-grit wheels. A 220-grit would be the very coarsest to use, and even this is too rough when cutting fairly small gems. If you are cutting on one of the 3M diamond-cabbing discs or faceting discs, the 220-disc is safe. You will find, however, that the 45-micron discs will cut as fast as you need, and produce a much smoother surface with much less shocking.

Shape the top of the stone a little at a time, frequently examining it for color display. You may change the orientation slightly as you go to take advantage of a band of color exposed by your work. This will necessitate changing the angle of the base, so you cannot make too drastic a change in orientation or you will have to sacrifice too much material when bringing the base back to flat under the new top position. Small corrections are permissible, however, and you should never hesitate to change direction for the improvement of the gem. The fact that you have to repeat your labor of basing the stone, removing it from the dop and redopping it, should not prevent your making any change that clearly will be an improvement.

The instructions provided with their kits by the Queensland Opal Cutters advocate grinding and sanding dry or nearly dry, while I have stressed the point so far of using an abundance of coolant. This seeming paradox is easily explained. Dry cutting saves a lot of time, and if you are cutting commercially, you should certainly take advantage of any shortcuts possible to save time and labor. However, if you are doing commercial cutting, then you have the experience needed to anticipate every possible pitfall in cutting opal and are well equipped to perform dry cutting. Since this book is dedicated to the beginner as well as the experienced cutter, I give directions that are safer, rather than faster, and the experienced cutter will as a matter of course ignore those precautions which are unnecessary for him.

When an opal is cut dry, the stone heats up far faster than it does under ample coolant. The great advantage of dry cutting is the revelation of every tiny flaw and crack, which otherwise would be hidden or filled when water or oil is used. Dust is also a factor in dry cutting, and some provision must be made to wipe the surface of the stone frequently. Since you must examine it frequently, you can at the same time wipe it on a piece of sponge or even on the seat of your work pants. A swipe across the stone is all that is needed to remove the dust from the surface.

Cutting under a coolant requires that the stone be dried before each examination, and the wiping of the moisture from the surface does not suffice. The water entering any crack present will hide that crack from view, and unless the stone is *really* dry, you will be apt to miss the flaw. An answer to the dilemma of waiting for a couple of hours every time you want to examine the progress of your work is solved by having several stones in the same stage of work. These need not all be opals, although it would be grand to be able to cut a dozen or more of these highly desirable gems at a sitting.

When you have ground a bit and want to examine the progress of the opal, wipe it as dry as you can, then stand the dopstick in a warm place to permit the complete drying of the stone, and during the waiting time, grind the other gems.

You will find, after you have cut a few gemstones, that it does not pay to set up an operation for just one stone, but you will collect several together and take them all at the same time through the several stages of production. This not only gives you the opportunity to let an opal dry out for inspection, but it breaks the monotony of working a long time on the same gem. However, I cannot imagine the cutting of any stone being a monotonous procedure, since every stone is individual, unique, and a new sensation of accomplishment.

During the grinding to shape—called roughing-out, by the way—the small flats occurring during the grinding stages should be removed as much as possible. There will always be some remaining, but these will disappear during the sanding operation. However, do not become lax in the grinding stage and leave flats and ridges that could be removed for the sanding stage. Take them out as far as you possibly can.

Sanding an Opal

In cutting any gemstone, the most important operation of the entire procedure is the sanding. Here the stone is smoothed to final shape, scratches are removed, and the surface is prepared for the final polishing. You will not be able to obtain a good polish on any stone that has been improperly sanded. Sanding may take as long to perform as all the other operations put together, but the time spent in sanding shows immediately when the stone is put to the polishing lap. A perfectly prepared surface and polish is the mark of a good craftsman, and in the case of opal, especially, good craftsmanship wants to be seen. The gem deserves the very best work you can bestow upon it.

In sanding with diamond belts on rubber expanding drums, two grades are used. The first, or coarse, sanding is done on 220-mesh belt, and the final, or fine, sanding on the 15-micron belt. With diamond, these two stages are all that are necessary to prepare the gem for the final polish.

If you are using silicon-carbide belts, then more stages are needed to obtain a good polishing surface. You may start with the 220-mesh belt, then down to a 400-mesh for intermediate sanding. After this, fine sanding is done on a 600-mesh belt, and then to a 1200-mesh belt if one is available. If not, the 600 may give you a surface smooth enough to polish if you sand first on the 600 mesh, then again on another 600 belt which has been worn fairly smooth. An old, worn 600 belt will perform much like a finer grade, but it will naturally cut much slower.

The stone should be kept moving at all times when in contact with the sanding belt. The curved surfaces should be smoothed out and faired into one another so that the entire top of the gem is a smooth transition from one side at the base to the other. If the stone is being cut as an ellipse, then both curves should blend with each other into a smoothly rounded top.

After all of the flats and ridges left by the grinding process have been removed on the coarse sanding belt, you may take the gem down to the fine belt which is used to remove all scratches left by the coarse one. Examine the surface under a glass rather than with the naked eye. This will reveal scratches not seen otherwise. Every single scratch left by the 220 belt must be removed before attempting to polish the gem. When you have sanded the stone to your satisfaction, the dop and the stone should be washed thoroughly to remove any grit or stone dust that may be imbedded.

Polishing an Opal

The polishing lap should be kept scrupulously clean, because one single grain of abrasive falling on the polishing plate will hopelessly scratch the surface of the gemstone, sometimes to the point where it will have to be ground and sanded all over again. The very least that can happen then is that the size of the stone is materially reduced, incurring a substantial loss of value in the case of opal or other precious material.

The finest polish is obtained on opal with the use of cerium oxide on a felt lap. However, I like to polish this wonderful gem in two stages, using tin oxide on canvas for the first polish. When the entire surface is brightly polished on the canvas lap, the dopstick and stone must again be washed thoroughly to remove every single trace of the polishing compound. A brush may be used for this operation to make certain it is done completely. Now the final polish is put on, using cerium oxide and a felt lap. The felt lap may be a thick felt wheel or a regular lap covered with thick felt sheeting.

The polishing machine sold by Duc-Kit, is ideal for the purpose, because the laps can be changed in a matter of seconds, and the lap plates themselves covered with any material you wish to use. A ¼-inch-thick felt disc cemented to one of these laps makes a perfect polishing lap for opal. The cerium oxide produces a liquid surface on the opal which brings out every single flake of color.

Making Opal Doublets

We come now to the problem of cutting a gemstone out of opal like the Australian black opal, which occurs as thin seams or veins in the matrix rock. Since a seam of this material thick enough to cut solid gems out of would cost several thousand dollars in the rough, we will disregard that practically unobtainable type for the more possible thin veins of color. If you can find and afford a piece having a vein ⅛ inch thick or close to it, you are fortunate indeed, since, with the aid of the thin-kerf saw you can slit the opal right through the middle of the vein to produce two gems, mirror images of each other, and cut perfectly matched pairs of stones from them.

Doublets are precious opals, occurring in thin veins, which have been cemented to a base of potch, agate, obsidian, or other mineral, leaving just a thin layer of opal showing on the top. The base is not seen when the gem is mounted in a setting, and when preparing the gemstone, a thin border of the base material is left around the edge for the prongs of the setting to grip, rather than turning them over on the opal itself, with the consequent danger of chipping the edge of the stone.

Cementing to the base is a fairly simple operation, but care must be taken to have all contacting surfaces perfectly flat and true. This is done in one of two ways. First, if the vein is thick enough to split down the middle, as mentioned above, then the opal surfaces exposed by the slitting-saw cut are lapped perfectly flat and cemented to the base.

First, the prepared stones are positioned on a plate of quartz to obtain the best fit.

Mark lines on the quartz plate to fit each stone, and also to act as guidelines for sawing the sheet into individual sections.

When cutting doublets, mark the shape and size with a template on the quartz backing plate.

Now the stones are fastened to the quartz plate with epoxy cement.

Clamp each piece with a wooden spring clothespin, making sure the stone and the doublet plate do not slide apart.

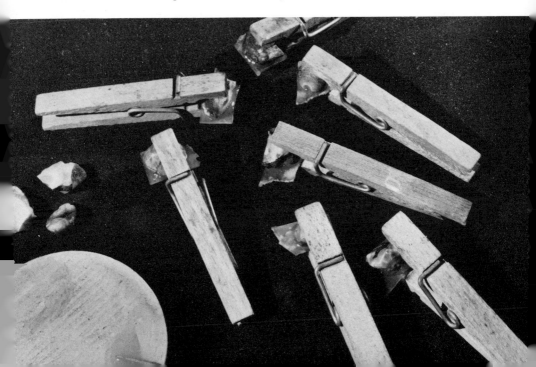

The surfaces are prepared best by lapping on a fine grade of 3M faceting disc. A 45-micron or 15-micron disc would be suitable for this purpose. If you do not have such a disc, you must lap the surface on a true and accurate grinding wheel, as fine as possible, or on a steel or copper lap using loose abrasive grains of silicon carbide. 400-grit would be good for this purpose. The grit is used with water or oil as a lubricant.

One surface of the doublet material for the base must also be lapped as carefully as the opal. When both surfaces are prepared, they should be washed with a detergent, rinsed with clear water, and dried thoroughly before joining them together. The best cement for this purpose is black epoxy. Clear epoxy can be used on opaque material, but if the opal is translucent, use either black epoxy or stain the bottom surface of the opal black. There are stains available for this purpose. Of course, the use of black base material would eliminate the need of staining the opal, if you cannot find any black epoxy at your lapidary supply company. Black obsidian would be good here.

The opal and the base material should be warmed, then a thin coating of epoxy spread on one or the other. Take care to eliminate every tiny air bubble that may be present in the adhesive, then place the opal on top of the base and rub them together with a slight pressure to make certain all the air is expelled from between the two surfaces. Set aside to cure.

If the material you are working has veins of color so thin that they are impossible to slit down the middle, then the operation is slightly different. The potch or rock on one side of the vein of color is carefully cut away on the slitting saw, then the sawed surface is lapped down until the opal is exposed. From now on the operations are identical: the preparation of both surfaces, cementing, and curing.

You now have one or more pieces of material, cemented to a layer of base material, and you are ready to cut your gems. Whether you slit a vein of color down the middle or cut away the potch from one side of a thinner vein, the pieces will now look the same: an opal side cemented to a base material. The next step is carefully to cut away the potch from the outside of the vein, exposing, or nearly exposing, the opal once again. It is better to make the saw cut a fraction of an inch out from the opal layer and grind down to that, rather than to try to cut right at the beginning of the color.

The next operation is to saw away the excess base material, making this cut parallel to the opal face. A good method of producing a parallel cut is to fasten the mineral to a square block of wood with a drop of epoxy cement. There is an epoxy on the market which sets up in about five minutes, and this is good for your purpose. Now the block of wood can be secured in the saw clamp with the face to which the stone is cemented parallel to the saw blade. The cut may now be made with greater accuracy than if the stone were held in the fingers while sawing.

The stone is removed from the wood block with solvent, or the wood can be sawed off the stone, leaving a thin layer of wood which you may sand off by hand. An examination of the stone should be made to check the parallelism of the two surfaces, and any irregularity should be lapped off on a flat lap until both surfaces are truly plane and parallel.

After sawing away the potch, you should mark the outline of the gem on the freshly sawed surface, and holding the stone in your fingers, grind the outside edges to shape and size. If the stone is so small that you cannot hold it in your fingers, then you can dop it up on a thin dopstick and grind the edges to shape and size.

Now the shaped stone should be dopped up with the opal side toward the wax, leaving the base exposed for working. You must make certain that the stone is attached to the dopstick perfectly square with the end of the stick—or, I should say, perpendicular to the length of the stick, since the end need not necessarily be square to the axis. This is best done in a dopping jig, but if you have a good eye and a steady hand, it may be done without a mechanical aid. The base should be ground down until it is about 1/16 inch thick. The thickness will increase a bit with larger stones and decrease slightly with smaller stones, 1/16 inch being about average for a stone of around 15 × 20 mm. The surface of the base must be very slightly domed or rounded, not perfectly flat. This will enable you to produce a better polish on it. Now the entire edge should be beveled to about 25 or 30 degrees, with the bevel slanting in from the edge at the opal line.

After grinding the base surface and the bevel, sand the stone and polish it exactly as though it were the opal itself. This is to say, take as much time and care to sand and polish the base as you are going to take for the top of the gem.

You must now remove the stone from the dopstick and dop it again, this time with the opal layer exposed for work. This is a tricky operation, because the stone must be dopped back with the base exactly perpendicular to the axis of the dopstick, and the surface of the base will be hidden the moment it touches the dopping wax.

The simplest way to accomplish the transfer of sides is to use a transfer jig, such as a faceting lapidary uses, or a version thereof. A transfer jig is a device into which a dopping stick is clamped with the stone in place. A second dopping stick is placed into the other side of the jig and pushed up against the stone. The second dopstick has a gob of hot wax on it. The stone is dopped between two sticks, held exactly in line with each other. You can now cut the wax off the stone on the side of the original dopstick to free it, assured that the stone is in exactly the same relative position on the new dopstick.

A simple transfer jig can be made out of a couple of blocks of steel and a length of angle iron welded to them. The blocks are first welded or bolted to a base plate, then the angle iron is welded to the blocks. After the welding is completed, the center is cut out of the angle iron to make the space for the stone. This jig is not accurate enough for transferring faceted stones, but it will be quite accurate enough for cabochon cutting.

After the stone has been transferred to the new dopstick, you may finish the opal on top. If there is any potch or matrix rock covering the opal, this must be ground away. Make frequent examinations as you grind, and as soon as the color shows, check the entire surface to make sure that the layer of opal has been exposed. If not, grind a little more, stopping every few seconds to examine the result. As soon as the color has been freed over the entire surface, stop grinding and carry the stone to the sander.

The top should be sanded flat instead of crowned as you did the base. When the sanding is completed, you must cut a very narrow chamfer around the edge until the base material is touched. This will place the base material all around the edge, and when the stone is set in a piece of jewelry, the setting will fasten to the base material, eliminating the possibility of chipping the edge of the opal.

Polish the gem on canvas with tin oxide first, then finish it up on a felt lap charged with cerium oxide to put the liquid surface on the gem. Be sure to polish the chamfer as well as the top of the stone.

JADE

Jade is another gem material that is said to be hard to work. Actually, I have not found it all that difficult. True, jade is stringy and tough, and the shaping of gemstones from it takes more time and care than do stones from agate, for example. However, it grinds very easily on diamond tools, and polishes readily on a leather lap with Raybright A, or on a canvas lap with tin oxide. Sometimes a better polish results if you use the tin oxide first, then finish up the gloss on leather. Use the laps almost dry when putting on the final gloss.

Jadeite and nephrite are the two minerals classed together as *jade*. Of the two, nephrite is the better quality, and this mineral is found in huge deposits in the Frazer River Valley in British Columbia and in Alaska, as well as in several other states in this country and in Europe.

The main difficulty most amateurs experience in cutting jade is the bad habit it has of undercutting when it is sanded or polished. This can be alleviated somewhat by using diamond all the way when working the stone. Diamond cuts so readily that practically no pressure against the disc or belt is required to remove material. Thus the undercutting is practically eliminated when cutting with diamond. Undercutting is caused by the fibrous construction of the mineral and by areas of material less tough than the main body. This weaker substance pulls right out of the stone, leaving pits and wavy indentations, if too much pressure is applied when either sanding or polishing. While jade is insensitive to heat, still the very lightest touch should be used in working it.

Also, jade does not take the brilliant liquid surface when it is polished that obsidian does, for example. Instead it acquires a soft gleam that is characteristic of the mineral, and which is very beautiful in itself. So do not force your stone on the polishing lap, trying to achieve the impossible; this is merely another cause of undercutting.

Jade is a tough, durable material and, because of its fibrous quality, ideally adapted to carving. Oriental craftsmen make use of much of this mineral for their delicate carved jars, vases, and ornaments. Some of the most ornate carvings in existence are made either of nephrite or jadeite by the able Chinese craftsmen, and this work has been done for centuries.

One of the difficulties in cutting jade is the fact that the qualities of the mineral will vary from piece to piece. One piece will grind perfectly, sand nicely under a wet sander, and polish with little or no difficulty. The next time you cut jade, the piece may evidence completely different qualities — undercutting persistently with a wet sanding belt, and pitting and pulling on the polishing lap. This piece should be tried on a dry sanding belt, and an almost dry lap, substituting a harder polishing surface for the one first used. If you polished the first gem on canvas, try leather for the one that pulls. If leather was used for the easily worked one, then try a soft wood lap for the one that undercuts so readily.

A certain amount of common sense must be used when circumstances like this arise, but the main point I am trying to bring out is that jade, unlike most other minerals, cannot be typed into a regular routine in cutting procedure. Each piece must be treated as it demands, rather than cut to specifications followed in the first cutting. Naturally, all the gemstones cut from one single piece of jade will exhibit the same or nearly the same characteristics, and all these gems can be cut and polished with the same routine. It is the challenge of working jade that makes up part of the appeal it has for lapidaries the world over.

Excellent results are sometimes obtained by sanding and polishing jade on the plastic Ultralap discs on the Ray-Tilt gem-cutting machine. The first cutting should be done on the grinding wheel, using a 220 or finer stone. The first sanding is done either on the 220-mesh diamond belt or a silicon-carbide belt of the same grade. Then the stone is sanded on the Ultralap discs, progressing from the coarsest to the finest, and finally to the polishing discs, starting with tin oxide and then switching to a chrome-oxide disc for the final polish. If the gem undercuts with the discs, try using them on a lap without the rubber backing. Peel the rubber sheet from one disc and cement the Ultralap directly to the metal surface, having first cleaned the surface of any specks of adhesive that remain after the rubber is removed.

A wooden polishing lap is easily made to fit the Ray-Tilt from a piece of ½-inch-thick hard maple, sawed or turned to a 6-inch-diameter disc, and drilled in the exact center to accept a short ½-inch 20-thread carriage bolt. This bolt, screwed into the shaft of the Ray-Tilt arbor, will hold the wooden disc securely during rotation. The disc may be charged with Raybright A or any other abrasive you want to use. Naturally enough, you would not use more than one kind of abrasive on each wooden disc.

MAKING CABOCHONS
FROM OTHER PRECIOUS STONES

Some other precious minerals that are used for making cabochon stones are ruby, emerald (usually when it is flawed too much to facet), tourmaline, star garnet, and some of the synthetics like Linde sapphire. There are many more, but these are very popular and within the limits of a modest pocketbook. Ruby and emerald are no trouble to cut and polish, but they are very hard, and the cutting is extremely slow on abrasive tools other than diamond. Still, much good work can be done with silicon-carbide tools.

When cutting star or asteriated minerals, you have another thing to contend with. The mineral must be oriented correctly in order to reveal the star. This is also true of tourmaline, which should be oriented in order to show color, since much tourmaline is dichroic, appearing as one color from one direction and as another from a different direction. Tourmaline should be oriented so that the top of the stone faces the side of the crystal from which it is cut when the mineral is of the blue or green varieties, and the top of the stone facing one end of the original crystal when cutting the pink variety. In other words, the base of the gem should be parallel to the side of the crystal for blue and green, and parallel to the end of the crystal when cutting the pink kind. This will give you the most intense color.

The rough mineral of any of the precious-gem materials should be examined carefully for flaws before cutting. It would be a shame to cut a beautiful cabochon from a crystal only to have it separate into two or more fragments at some stage of the cutting process. It is even worse if the stone holds together only until you begin to set it into an article of jewelry. Italdo Originals, makes two kinds of refraction-detector fluids, Refractol and star Refractol. Refractol is used to expose the flaws in transparent rough-cutting minerals. To use Refractol, simply immerse the crystal in the jar of fluid and examine it under a strong incandescent light. When a flaw is detected, you should note the position within the crystal, and try to cut your gem to miss the fracture. If this is simply impossible to do, then what you should try for is to "lock" the fracture. This means cut the gem so that, while the fracture enters the stone, it does not pass clear through it, but ends only partway into the finished gem. This will keep the gem from separating into fragments at least, and some minerals look all right even if they do contain a fracture or two.

Some garnets, the Linde synthetic sapphires (and natural ones, too), some rose quartz, and many other minerals often show asteriation in the form of a four-pointed star or a six-pointed star. This asteriation is caused by closely packed fibers in the crystal, oriented according to the different axes of the crystal. When the mineral is properly oriented with regard to the position of these fibers, the star appears as a chatoyancy on the surface of the gem, moving across the face of the gem as it is rotated or tipped. Tigereye is another mineral which shows this chatoyancy to a marked degree, although not in the form of stars.

At times it is very difficult to make certain of the orientation of a piece of rough mineral, and since the rough is rather expensive, you should take considerable time and care to make sure the rough is "right side up" before you begin to cut it. Star Refractol is a boon to lapidaries working asteriated minerals. A drop of this viscous liquid is placed on the rough and viewed in a strong incandescent light. If no star is visible, place another drop in another location on the rough, working your way around the piece until the asteriation is revealed. Bear in mind that the star will be very tiny, showing only on the drop of Star Refractol, not on the mineral, so look very closely, moving the stone slowly as you view it, to make the star move. The motion of the chatoyant star will call your attention to it more readily.

If any of the natural crystal faces are visible on the rough, they will give you a starting point. Place the rough with one of these faces down as a tentative base of the gem, and try the Star Refractol on the opposite or upper side. A slight rotation one way or another should reveal the desired play of asteriation. Once you have located the star—and if the piece of rough is large enough—sand and polish a "window" on the top. This window must have a domed shape, similar to the final shape of the cabochon you are going to cut. Now, after polishing, examine the gem. The star should be brilliant and readily observable in ordinary light. What you are doing now is checking whether or not you had the rough oriented correctly. If the star is exactly centered in the dome, it is properly positioned, and now you can flatten the base, dop the rough, and proceed to cut your gem. If the star is tipped slightly one way or another, then you should tip the stone to correct your preliminary orientation and go on from there. It takes time and patience to orient star minerals, but certainly the result is worth it. Such stones are valuable, as well as beautiful and interesting.

Beads made from asteriated minerals are lovely and show two distinct stars, one on each side of the bead. They should be drilled perpendicularly to the stars so that the stars will show movement as the beads rotate on their string when worn. A necklace of star garnets can be worth many hundreds or even thousands of dollars.

11.

Making
Rings and Bracelets

Many minerals lend themselves well to the fashioning of rings and bracelets without the addition of precious metals—silver, gold, or platinum. The best materials are those which are tough and not too susceptible to shock damage.

Jade is a good material for making rings and bracelets, and the cutting of these articles can be done with diamond or abrasive hole cutters. These are called core drills, and as such are made in a large variety of sizes. Of course, the diamond-core drills cut faster and more accurately, and outlast several abrasive drills. They also cost more, but this is offset by their longer life.

A core drill with an outside diameter the same as your ring size is used for cutting the center of a ring. A second core drill having an inside diameter of the center plus twice the thickness of the shank should be used for cutting the outside. This means, to clarify the preceding statement, that if you want to make a ring with a hole ⅝ inch in diameter and the ring itself ⅛ inch thick, you would use a ⅝-inch- diameter core drill for the center, and a ⅞-inch-diameter core drill for the outside.

In making a ring or a bracelet, it is wise to cut the larger, outside diameter first. This will produce a pancake-like blank on which it will be far easier to center the hole for the inside. If you cut the inside hole first, you will have to attempt to center the

196

larger drill over the hole without being able to see the inside hole, and this is very difficult.

Grinding and polishing the outer surfaces and the sides of the ring are easily performed with your regular equipment, holding the stone in your fingers. It is not necessary to dop it up.

The inside is another matter, as are the edges leading down into the bore. These should be smoothly rounded and polished. The very best tool for performing this work is a Foredom Flexible Shaft Tool. There are many models of these versatile machines and many different types of chucks, from key-type adjustable chucks to precision collets. Foredom makes the shafts in table models, as well as in conventional hanging types. I personally prefer the hanging kind, since the bench models take up room on my always-cluttered jewelry bench. However, you have a choice, since both perform ably and easily.

Small diamond-tipped carving tools are the best and easiest to use in the Foredom Flexible Shaft, and the ring can be held either in your fingers or in a clamp of any convenient kind. A small vise with the jaws covered by bending a piece of sheet lead around them will serve to hold a jade blank firmly while you work the inside. Use the largest tools possible when cutting the edges and inside. You will be less likely to make ridges in the mineral that will have to be ground or sanded out before the ring is polished.

Sanding can be done on small hard felt discs in mandrels placed in the Foredom Flexible Shaft Tool and charged with silicon-carbide abrasive powder. Better is to use one of the diamond-powder pastes on felt discs, and still better is a diamond spray. 3M and other companies manufacture paste-diamond polishes put up in syringes from which small quantities can be dispensed. Keep the felt discs apart when using more than one size of abrasive. Also, keep them identified in some fashion, so you can use them again when needed.

The diamond spray is made by Italdo and is supplied in various grades ranging from $1/4$ micron to 25 microns in particle size. The product is put up in sturdy bottles, each bottle containing a carat of diamond powder in a solution under pressure, as in an aerosol spray. While you rotate the felt disc slowly in the Foredom machine, shake the bottle vigorously to suspend the diamond powder completely in the solution and spray it on the felt. It's as easy as that.

Abrasive powders are also supplied in paste form by Raytech under the name Raybide, in several grades ranging from 100 grit to 28,000 grit. These, too, are useful as polishing material to be used on felt discs in the Foredom Flexible Shaft.

Bracelets are made exactly the same way as are rings, but the core drills must be considerably larger. You must be able to slip your hand through the hole made by the drill. The outside diameter of a bracelet may be cut by trimming on the Preformer saw and grinding to shape on a wheel, or it may be cut with a larger core drill as you do the rings. For that matter, the outside of a ring may be cut by hand, too, but the core drill is much faster and more accurate. In the ring sizes, diamond core drills are not prohibitive in cost, but in the very large diameters used for bracelets, they are quite expensive.

Abrasive core drills can also be used. They will cut all right, but the process is slow and a bit messy. The slice of jade is positioned below the drill and a well of some material or other is stuck to it surrounding the area to be drilled. The well may be made of paraffin wax, beeswax, modeling clay, potter's clay (damp), or any other material which will stick tightly to the surface of the stone and resist dissolving in water. This well should be deep enough — not less than ½ inch, I would say — to contain a fair amount of water to act as a coolant, and also to contain abrasive powder, which does the actual cutting.

Abrasive core drills are merely short sections of steel, brass, copper, or stainless steel tubing, welded to a mandrel to fit the chuck of an ordinary drill press. The mounting of the mandrel must be accurate, or the drill will wobble in the chuck. It must run perfectly true to cut properly. Usually the cutting end is notched all around the diameter. This can be done with a hack saw if you are making your own drills, and the spacing of the notches can be approximately equal, but this is not important. The purpose of the notches is to pick up and carry the abrasive powder to provide cutting action all around the diameter.

A drop or two of Photoflo solution obtainable in any photo-supply store or a pinch of powdered detergent in the water inside the well will act as a wetting agent and keep the abrasive grains in suspension a little better than if just plain water is used. The only trouble with using detergent rather than Photoflo is the possibility of foaming. Too much foam will hide the work area and you cannot see what you are doing. Abrasive core drills, which are sometimes called *mud drills,* cut very slowly, and it helps speed up the work if you keep brushing the abrasive grains into the side of the drill as it revolves, to make sure that the notches are picking it up and distributing it evenly around the cut. A slight pressure must be maintained on the drill—just enough to permit cutting action to take place. You will be able to feel the cutting as you go, and soon will be able to judge the correct amount of pressure to use for the different sizes of drills.

The wax well is used on the stone when diamond core drills are used, too, and they are also filled with water. However, that is all that is used in diamond cutting. No abrasive is to be added. The detergent or Photoflo can still be used, if you wish, so that the liquid will wash away the chips a little easier.

Every few seconds the drill should be raised for a few revolutions, then once again lowered into the cut. This is to clear away any chips or slurry gathered under the cutting edge of the drill. This action is even more important when a diamond drill is being used, because the cutting edge of a diamond drill must be kept sharp and clean of debris.

Care should be taken when the saw breaks out through the bottom. If the slice of mineral is placed on a sheet of rubber, perhaps a piece cut from an old innertube, the breakthrough shock will be absorbed somewhat. At any rate, as soon as you feel the drill cutting through the bottom, lessen the pressure very slowly and feel your way very carefully through the last bit of mineral. To push the drill on through at the same cutting rate is only inviting trouble. Large flakes of material can snap off as the drill penetrates, and some of these flakes may be large enough to impinge on the area making the sides of the bracelet or ring. You would then have to grind the piece narrower by the amount of the lowest level of the flake, risking the possibility of ruining the article by making it too thin.

12.

Making
Spheres and Beads

When one of my sons was a schoolboy, he kept asking me for money to buy marbles. Time after time I was required to hand out a quarter or half-dollar for the purchase of another sack of "glassies" or other kinds of marbles. Finally, I asked him what in the world he was doing with all these things. The reply was startling. "I'm losing a lot of them," he told me. "But then, I'm winning a lot of others."

This didn't really make too much sense to me at the time, but I did not give it too much thought until one day my son walked into the house grinning from ear to ear. Then the story came out. It seems he had been playing marbles very seriously, training himself for the Great Marble Tournament of the area. It seems, also that he evidently took his marble shooting seriously, because he was the proud winner of the tournament, with a small gold medal to show for his prowess!

"Well," said I, "this calls for some kind of celebration. What would you like as your reward for the championship?"

"I'd like a real agate shooter, Dad."

"You shall have it. Just as soon as I can find one for you."

Little did I realize what I had let myself in for. After some days of fruitless searching around hobby shops and toy stores for an agate shooter, I was directed to an enormous sporting-goods firm. I was escorted to a counter upon which the clerk placed a velvet-lined tray with rows of pockets, in each of which reposed a gleaming sphere of agate. Mirror-polished, they varied slightly in size, and each one was a riot of color, each one different from its neighbor. They were indeed beautiful, and I could readily see why my boy wanted one.

I selected two of the most beautiful, one a little smaller than the other, as I knew that boys often liked a "knuckle shooter" in preference to a regular shooter. "How much?" The clerk finished returning the tray to the case, locking the sliding door. That should have been my clue to turn and dash madly from the premises. But I stood my ground, and the man said with a smile, "Twenty-five dollars."

I swallowed. Keeping a tight control on my expression and the frozen toothy smile on my lips, I slowly reached for my wallet, as the clerk continued, "Each." I paid and then endured the further indignity of having to shell out sales tax as well.

Those shooters stuck in my craw for a long, long time. Not any more, though. Now I am a lapidary, and I have made spheres and beads for myself. If I were affluent enough, I would like to go back to that store and hand the clerk a couple of hundred dollars, announcing that he had grossly undercharged me for the two marbles.

SPHERES

Sphere making is a long and tedious job. The result is well worth the effort, but the first sphere will drive you batty. Actually, the mechanics of making spheres are not all that complicated. It only takes time and patience, and you must have a machine which will, with a minimum of trouble, produce a perfect ball from a chunk of intractable mineral.

Alfred Bernstein Enterprises makes a simple and very effective sphere machine. The machine incorporates three grinding heads, each individually driven by a slow-speed motor. Mr. Bernstein recommends nine different steps for the production of spheres, which steps will be outlined here, after some preliminary information of my own.

In order to make a sphere, you must have massive pieces of rough. By massive, I mean solid, free from fractures and blemishes, and large enough to make a sphere the size you want. The Bernstein machine will make spheres ranging from about 1½ inches in diameter to about 4 inches in diameter. Many minerals used for gem cutting do not come in large enough pieces to make spheres of any size. Many of them do, however, and these are the ones we will discuss.

One of the very best minerals for grinding spheres is obsidian. This is available in lumps weighing many pounds, and the mineral is usually free of fractures and pits or voids. Agate is also found in large enough pieces to make good-sized spheres, as is quartz, especially rose quartz, but this mineral is also usually full of fractures, so you must hunt around for good rough before you make a selection. Onyx is a good mineral for a sphere, and it comes in enormous masses. A septarian nodule makes a most beautiful and unusual sphere when it is ground down far enough to expose the inner filling of calcite, goethite, or other mineral, as well as some of the outer hardened clay covering.

Whatever mineral you choose, the first step is to cut it into a cube with sides just slightly larger than the sphere you wish to make. By slightly larger, I mean just that — not more than ⅛ inch larger, and preferably a little less. Let us assume that you are going to make a 2½-inch sphere. You will want to produce a 2⅝-inch cube of the mineral being used.

Now all eight corners are cut off the cube, in the form of triangular pyramids, leaving the dimension between the cuts the same as the original dimension of the cube — that is, 2⅝ inches. In order to cut the corners off the cube, it may be necessary for you to make a couple of vee blocks out of wood to clamp the cube in your saw vise. Incidentally, save the corners as you cut them off. They can be ground to uniform size and tumble-polished, and will make a most unusual and interesting necklace.

You now have produced a figure having 14 sides—the six faces of the original cube, plus the eight faces produced by cutting off the corners. The dimensions from all directions across opposite faces should be the same—in this case, 2⅝ inches.

The next step is to grind all the sharp corners off the cube on a coarse, 100-grit wheel. You should shape the block on the wheel to as nearly spherical as possible, but do not grind any material off the flat faces. Only the ridges at the corners should be taken away. The more nearly you round the block the easier it will be to grind the sphere in the machine.

You now place the more or less lopsided sphere in the machine. Adjust all the heads so they suspend the ball in the center of the machine, with all heads at more or less the same angle. Raise the grit container until it just touches the bottom of the ball. Charge the holder with number 80-mesh silicon-carbide powder and a lubricant. Mr. Bernstein recommends one part #10 motor oil and two parts kerosene. I have used this, and also plain water with a drop of wetting agent such as Photoflo solution. Both work well. As the machine grinds the lump into a perfect sphere, make sure that there is enough grit and lubricant at all times in the abrasive carrier. A small brush will help move the grit up onto the surface of the mineral if it fails to pick up itself. At no time should the mineral run dry.

A very important thing to watch is the movement of the lump in the machine. As the mineral is ground, it must revolve constantly in all directions. The heads of this particular machine are held in place with a heavy rubber band snapped around all three motor arms. If the mineral revolves only in one direction, a second rubber band snapped over only two of the heads will place tension on those heads, causing the mineral to change direction in its rotation. By experimenting with varying tensions, moving the rubber band from one pair of heads to the other, you will be able to adjust the tension to the point where the ball revolves in all directions as it is supposed to do. This is a very important part of sphere grinding, since it follows that unless the mineral is revolved so that every part of the surface is brought under the grinding heads, it will not be ground into a perfect sphere. Also, you should pay attention to getting an equal amount of abrasive under each grinding head at all times. The brush will help do this for you, but you must stand watch as the work progresses to see if it is necessary.

Stop the machine to examine the progress from time to time. The grinding operation will take anywhere from four to five hours to two or three days, depending on the size of the sphere being ground and the hardness of the material from which it is being made. The grinding will be completed when the sphere shows that every flat surface of the lump has been ground by the heads. Each surface will present a flat circle as the grinding progresses, and these circles will become smaller and smaller as more material is removed. When the last circle disappears the grinding is finished, and the sphere may be removed from the machine and thoroughly cleaned.

Now the machine itself must be completely cleaned of *every single grain of abrasive*. I cannot stress too much the importance of that last statement. If *one single grain* of abrasive remains in or on any of the heads, or on the machine where it can fall into the heads, the next step will be lost and the work will have to be started all over again. This means that the abrasive carrier must also be as clean as the rest of the machine. As a matter of fact, I have found that cleaning the abrasive carrier is an almost impossible task, so I make a series of carriers and label them for the different grits used. Then, as each step is begun, the carrier is changed for the one before it. Since the carriers are nothing more than a small tunafish can with a piece of sheet plastic stretched loosely over the open end, they are easy to make. Each can is fastened to a short length of wooden dowel by driving a small nail through the center of the can into the end of the dowel.

When you are certain that the machine, grinding heads, carrier, and surrounding area are free of all abrasive used, you may charge the carrier with 220-grit powder and repeat the grinding operation. A hint here will not be amiss. Before you begin the second grinding operation, examine all the grinding heads. Sometimes you will find a burr or paper-thin edge loose on a head. This must be filed or ground away before the head is put into use, or this edge may come loose and scratch the sphere so badly that you will have to start all over to remove the scratches. Three or four hours should be enough for the machine to remove all the scratches put into the mineral by the 80-mesh. The surface will now be covered with finer scratches and will appear much smoother than it did before. Remove the sphere from the machine, clean it thoroughly, and dry it. Now you can examine it under a magnifying glass to make sure all the coarse scratches have been ground away. They will stand out readily if they haven't, in which case you must return the sphere to the machine for further grinding.

After the 220 grind is completed, again you clean the machine, heads, and surrounding area completely of every grain of the 220 powder. Change the carrier to a new one and charge it with 600-mesh silicon carbide. The sphere now is ground in this third stage until all the scratches left by the 220 mesh are removed. The ball will now appear very smooth, and you can begin to get an idea of what it will look like when it is finished. Examine it under the glass, and when it is all ground to the 600 mesh, the operation is repeated with the next finer (and last) grinding operation.

If you were careful all the other times to get everything spotlessly clean, you must be doubly so now, because the 600-mesh powder is so fine that you might very well miss a few grains. It will only take one grain to spoil all the previous work, so take your time. You can remove the heads from their shafts and scrub them in a bath of kerosene, being careful to return them to their former position on the motor shaft. Wash down the motor-holding plates, hinges, carrier socket, and everything else with kerosene and a soft brush. Just make certain that everything is free of abrasive powder, then set it up and charge a new carrier with the last stage of abrasive—1200-mesh powder. At this point, though, you change the procedure somewhat.

For the 1200-mesh grinding, which is really a pre-polish operation, you must pad the grinding heads. Thick felt or heavy, soft leather is used for the purpose, and discs of this material must be cut large enough to cover the head, turning down over the sides. A strong rubber band may be snapped around the head to hold the pad in place, or a wire may be twisted around the head and the pad, holding it securely. Bend the ends of the wire down flat against the head so they will not catch on the abrasive carrier as it revolves. If leather is used, the flesh side should be out, rather than the hair side. The flesh side is covered with a slight nap which holds the polishing abrasive rather well.

Both felt and leather pad covers should be dampened before the grinding operation is begun, and they should be kept moist throughout the entire operation. Not wet, just damp. This is easily done by using an eyedropper to deposit a drop or two on each pad as the head revolves. You will see, from the surface of the sphere, when moisture is needed and can adjust the amount to suit the grinding action.

Each grinding stage will take from two to four hours. Sometimes a very hard piece of material will take longer. Brazilian agate is one material that may take twice as long at each grinding step. Between each step you should examine the grinding heads for burrs, removing any with a file or by grinding the edges of the heads. During each step you must be sure that the sphere is rotating in all directions under the heads, adjusting tensions as necessary with rubber bands.

Be more than usually critical in examining the last (1200) grinding stage, making certain that every single scratch is out of the sphere. Now, after cleaning and drying, it is ready for the polishing step.

The pads must be changed for the final polishing, and the heads thoroughly cleaned before new pads are installed. Tin oxide is the polish to be used for most materials. Some minerals will polish better with cerium oxide, but tin oxide is almost a universal polishing compound, so I would recommend using that at least at the start. If, after a reasonable amount of time in the machine, the tin oxide doesn't appear to be doing a good job, you may re-cover the heads and substitute cerium oxide, but I really do not think this will be necessary.

While you will be able to obtain an excellent polish on the surface of a sphere, you will never be able to achieve the truly liquid surface possible when polishing a cabochon, so do not strive for this goal. The reason is, of course, that the comparatively slow movement of the mineral in the polishing heads of a sphere-making machine do not generate enough heat to melt the surface as do the more rapid speed and greatly increased pressure of hand polishing against a canvas or leather lap.

Examine the sphere every couple of hours, cleaning and drying it first. When finally the surface is evenly polished and all scratches are gone, your work is over. Spheres have a special attraction for many persons, myself among them, and to me this is one of the most interesting phases of lapidary work. Also, a collection of spheres makes a most unusual mineral collection, showing the specimen off in splendor.

BEADS

Bead making is really a method of making diminutive spheres, but in the case of beads, several are ground simultaneously in the bead mill.

A bead mill is a simple enough piece of equipment. It consists of two circular plates, each having a groove cut into it, half-round in section, and perhaps ¼ inch deep, by ¾ inch wide. The plates are set so that the grooves face each other. The bottom plate is mounted on a base consisting essentially of a short section of tubing large enough to accommodate the plate inside, and three or four spring-loaded supporting bars. The bottom plate resting on these bars is able to float loosely, moving up or down as pressure is placed upon it. It is able also to tilt slightly, if the pressure on one side is unequal to the pressure on the other side. The top plate, identical in shape to the bottom plate, has a shaft secured to the center of the smooth side to enable it to be fastened in the chuck of a drill press.

The mineral to be made into beads is prepared much the same way as that used for making a sphere, except for size. The material is cut into small cubes first, then each cube is ground down to as near a ball as possible, holding the cube in the fingers

Mark squares on the slab equal in both directions to the thickness of the slab. This will produce cubes for bead making.

After the slab is cut into cubes, each cube is held in the fingers and ground into rough shape on a coarse wheel.

Grinding a bead blank into a roughly spherical shape preparatory to grinding it in a mill.

Above: A bead mill being loaded with the roughly ground bead blanks.

Opposite: The bead mill in operation. It will grind a full load of about 20 beads to a spherical shape in about 20 minutes. Then the beads can be polished in a tumbler.

and using a 100-grit grinding wheel. The corners are ground off rather than sawed off, since it would be difficult to clamp such small sections in a saw vise, and anyway, the hand grinding is much faster.

When you have a number of pieces prepared, they are distributed around the groove in the bottom plate, and lubricant and 80-grit abrasive powder are placed in the groove with the blanks. In a mill having a 6-inch-diameter plate, a proper charge would be about 20 bead blanks.

The quill of the drill press is lowered until a slight pressure is placed on the bottom plate, being taken up by the spring-loaded supports. Now the press is started, running on its lowest speed. Every few minutes you should stop the machine, lift the top plate and examine the blanks; they should be grinding into perfect balls. To do so, they must rotate freely within the grooves of the plates under slight pressure. As soon as the beads are round, you may begin to graduate them if desired. This is simple. As soon as the beads are perfectly round and of a size desired for the largest bead in a necklace, remove one bead, then continue grinding the remainder. When the beads are ground down to the second size, remove *two* beads. Grind smaller and remove two more, repeating this operation until you reach the size of the smallest beads on the string. Always stop grinding when the bead is just the smallest fraction larger than you wish the finished bead to be.

When all the beads have been formed in the mill, you can tumble-polish them, exactly as you tumble-polish fragments of minerals. Chapter 7 will give you the exact steps to take in this operation.

If you wish to drill your own beads, you must have a bead gripper. This is a special type of clamp sold in lapidary supply houses for a small sum, and it will hold the round bead firmly while you drill it with a diamond drill. It is a good idea to drill halfway through, then reverse the bead, placing it on the guide post in the clamp, and drill the other half, meeting in the middle. This way, the mineral does not fracture at the point of exit, as might otherwise occur.

If you prefer, you may drill the beads before tumble-polishing them, but this produces two hazards. One, the bead wears away around the hole on both sides, making the holes slightly funnel-shaped. Sometimes this will not matter, especially if you intend to use rondelles between each bead. Rondelles are thin wafers of clear quartz, faceted around the edges and drilled through the center. They are used to separate beads when stringing them. It is far cheaper to buy rondelles already made than to try to make them yourself. They are manufactured in Europe and cost only a few cents each. Any gem dealer should have them for sale.

The other hazard, and a far more serious one to my mind, is that the hole will pack up with abrasive powder and slurry during each tumbling operation, and there is the very great possibility of not getting all the grit out of every bead. This will result in calamity, because when the next finer stage is undertaken, the grit remaining in the hole of only one bead is enough to scratch the surfaces of every bead in the tumbler, necessitating your redoing the entire process.

If you do not wish to drill your own beads, there are several lapidary companies throughout the country that do custom drilling. At the time of writing this book, one such company charges 35¢ per bead for drilling, and this seems to be a small enough charge for a job that is tedious to do yourself. These companies have commercial drills set up and to them it is routine to drill an assortment of beads.

OVAL BEADS

Oval beads are a little harder to make than round ones. The bead mill will not grind oval beads very well, since the action of the mill is to produce spheres instead of ellipses. About the best way to produce oval beads is to cut the blanks in the form of rectangles having the length and breadth of the bead size desired.

Mark the center of each blank, dop it on one end, and grind

the other end to shape. You might make a template with a parabolic curve to use as a gauge in sizing the stone as you grind it. After shaping one side, remove the stone from the dopstick and dop it again on the finished end, to permit grinding the remaining end to shape. This will have to be done for each bead, of course, and you will have to take pains to grind them uniformly.

After the grinding has been completed, the beads may be tumble-polished and drilled. Drilling oval beads takes longer than drilling round beads for the simple reason that there is more material to be drilled in the ovals. Also, it requires a bit more care in starting the hole, because, unlike a sphere, an oval bead must be drilled in one direction only and the hole cannot be off center. It does not matter where you start to drill on a spherical bead.

Books and Periodicals

How many times has some friend shown me a truly beautiful specimen of one mineral or other and told me something like "I got it right down on Catfish Creek," pointing down Main Street in the direction of our local stream. Down I'd go, knowing better, but eager to find some of the same. A full day later, returning home bug-bitten, bramble-torn, broken-nailed, and utterly exhausted, I would run into my informant once more and tell him where I had been. "Oh, you went to the wrong place. I found it about two miles farther upstream."

Fee-collecting sites are, of course, the answer to this frustrating problem. A list of known sites has been included in Chapter 5 for your convenience. There are many more, but I have included only those sites from which I have had actual information about the area sent me by the proprietor.

There are also many books available on collecting sites. For the most part, the general area is given in the book, and you must do considerable research in order to pinpoint the actual site. Such books are very useful for planning a vacation field trip, where you can drive to the general area and camp out for a couple of weeks or more, leisurely exploring the surrounding territory. Very often you will discover a field rich in material, and have a barrel of fun besides. Some of these books are:

215

American Gem Trails, by Richard M. Pearl. McGraw-Hill Book
   Co., 1221 Avenue of the Americas, New York, N.Y. 10019.
Gem Hunter's Guide, by Russell P. McFall. T. Y. Crowell Co., 666
   Fifth Avenue, New York, N.Y. 10022.
Gemstones of North America, by John Sinkankas. D. Van Nos-
   trand Company, 450 West 33rd St., New York, N.Y. 10001.
Western Gem Hunter's Atlas, by Cyril Johnson. Obtain from Cy
   Johnson, Box 288, Susanville, Calif. 96130.
The Book of Agates and other Quartz Gems, by Lelande Quick.
   Chilton Books Company, 401 Walnut St., Philadelphia,
   Penna. 19106.

Some books which pinpoint locations for collecting and will be
very useful for rock hunters looking for specific minerals are:

Gem Trails of Arizona, by Bessie W. Simpson. Gem Trail Publi-
   cations, P.O. Box 157, Glen Rose, Texas 76043.
Arizona Rock Trails, by Fred H. Bitner. Bitner's, Scottsdale, Ariz.
   85251.
Arizona Gem Trails, by J. Ellis Ransom. Gemac Corp., Box 808,
   Mentone, Calif. 92359.
Desert Gem Trails, by Mary F. Strong. Gembooks, Mentone, Calif.
   92359.
Gemstones and Minerals, by John Sinkankas. Van Nostrand
   Reinhold Company, 450 West 33rd St, New York, N.Y.
   10001
The Rock Collector's Nevada and Idaho, by Darold J. Henry.
   Gordon's, P.O. Box 4073, Long Beach, Calif. 90801.
Petrified Forest Trails, by J. Ellis Ransom. Gemac Corp., Box 808,
   Mentone, Calif. 92359.
New Gem Material Locations, by P. R. Hernandez. Highland
   Patton Rock and Mineral Club, 7217 San Francisco St., High-
   land, Calif. 92346.
Lake Superior Agate, by Theodore C. Vanasse. The Spring Valley
   Sun, Spring Valley, Wis. 54767.
Ten Rock Trips Near Needles, by M. McShan and C. More.
   McShan's Rock Shop, Box 22, Needles, Calif. 92363.
Colorado Gem Trails and Mineral Guide, by Richard M. Pearl.
   Sage Books, 2679 South York Street, Denver, Colo. 80210.

Successful Mineral Collecting and Prospecting, by Richard M. Pearl. McGraw-Hill Book Company, 1221 Avenue of the Americas, New York, N. Y. 10019.

Eastern Gem Trails, by F. and H. Oles. Gembooks, Mentone, Calif. 92359.

Field Guide to the Gems and Minerals of Mexico, by Paul W. Johnson. Gembooks, Mentone, Calif. 92359.

New Mexico Gem Trails, by Bessie W. Simpson. Gem Trail Publications, P.O. Box 157, Glen Rose, Texas 76043.

Midwest Gem Trails, by J. C. Zeitner. Gembooks, Mentone, Calif. 92359.

The Rock Hunter's Range Guide, by J. Ellis Ransom. Harper and Row, 10 East 53rd St., New York, N.Y. 10022

We Walk on Jewels, by Jean Blackmore. Seth Lowe Press, Rockland, Maine 04841.

Gem Trails of Texas, by Bessie W. Simpson. Gem Trail Publications, P.O. Box 157, Glen Rose, Texas 76043.

Mineral Guide to New England, by Phillip Morril. House of Color, Intervale, N.H. 03845.

Rockhound Guide to New York State, by W. A. Tervo. Exposition Press, Inc., 386 Park Avenue South, New York, N.Y. 10016.

A Rockhound's Guide to the Gems and Minerals of Oklahoma, by E. L. Gilmore. E. L. Gilmore, 1206 West 19th St., Tulsa, Okla. 74101.

Minerals of The St. Lawrence Valley, by G. Robinson and S. Alverson. George Robinson, 327 Franklin St., Ogdensburg, N.Y. 13669.

Northwest Gem Trails, by H. C. Dake. Gembooks, Mentone, Calif. 92359

Mineral Trails of New Jersey, by Robert Jackson. Robert Jackson, 543 Cleveland Avenue, Riverdale, N.J. 07457.

The Agate Book, by H. C. Dake. Gemac Corp., Box 808, Mentone, Calif. 92359.

There are, of course, many more books on this popular subject, and these may be found in rock shops throughout the country, as well as in larger book stores. A letter to the Chamber of Commerce in most of the larger cities will possibly reward you with list of collecting locations and even maps. Especially helpful are the Chambers of Commerce of the Western cities, which are rapidly becoming aware of the tourist value to their states in catering to rockhounds.

There are also several companies which publish maps for rockhounding. The lapidary magazines do this; also you might write to the Westwide Maps Company, 114 West Third, Los Angeles, Calif. 90013.

PERIODICALS

There are a few good magazines which provide information on rock and mineral collecting, and also on lapidary work. Some of them are:

Earth Science, P.O. Box 1357, Chicago, Ill. Bimonthly.
Gems and Minerals, P.O. Box 687, Mentone, Calif. Monthly.
Lapidary Journal, P.O. Box 518, Del Mar, Calif.
  Monthly, with a buyer's guide issued each April. A valuable
  reference source.
The Mineralogist. P.O. Box 808, Mentone, Calif. Bimonthly.
Rocks and Minerals, P.O. Box 29, Peekskill, N.Y. Bimonthly.

Some of these magazines have their own lists of books which they sell as a service to their readers. Each issue will list the available titles.

Glossary

While the experienced lapidary or rockhound will be familiar with the language used in the hobby, some beginners will find terms unfamiliar to them, and for this reason a few of the more unusual words are defined herewith.

adularescence The pale-bluish light seen in moonstone and other feldspars of the adularia variety.

asterism The presence of a "star" of either four or six rays on the surface of some gems. This effect is caused by a quantity of very thin hairs or fibers of foreign mineral being present in a transparent or translucent mineral. These needles are present in sets. If a stone possesses only one set, the resultant gem is called a cat's-eye. If two sets of needles are present, the gem will have a four-rayed star, and if three sets of needles are in the mineral, a six-rayed star will result. Care must be taken to orient the stone properly when cutting.

bead mill A mechanical device used for grinding gem mineral pieces into beads of uniform size. A mill will produce only round beads, and will only grind them to size. Polishing must be done in a tumbler.

bezel   The rim of metal surrounding a gemstone in a setting. It secures the stone to the piece of jewelry.

botryoidal   Resembling a bunch of grapes in shape; said of smoothly rounded masses of a mineral.

breccia   An aggregate of angular fragments of stone or mineral cemented together, usually with calcite or chalcedony.

cab   A short term meaning *cabochon*.

cabochon   A piece of mineral cut into a gemstone having a flat, or nearly flat, bottom and a smoothly rounded top. The method is commonly used for cutting opaque and semi-precious minerals, as distinguished from faceting, which is used for transparent and more costly minerals. There are exceptions to both these statements. Opals, a most precious mineral, usually is cut as a cabochon.

cameo   A carved gem, usually made from shell, but often cut from onyx or other mineral occurring in bands of different colors. The design is cut in such a way as to offer the relief work in one color against a background of contrasting color. Most shell cameos are carved in Italy. The opposite of *intaglio*.

chatoyancy   The property of a gemstone that shows a movable bar or star of light on its surface, due to the inclusion of foreign minerals. See *asterism*.

core drill   A tubular drill used for removing fairly large sections of material. Often used for cutting mineral rings and bracelets, drilling slabs for desk pens and pencils, etc. Made either in diamond tip or plain to be used with abrasive grains.

dichroic   Possessing the property of showing two different colors when viewed from two different angles. Tourmaline is an excellent example of dichroism.

dike In the forming of rocks, basalt, when intruding sedimentary rocks in a vertical or nearly vertical position, is called a *dike.*

dop, dopstick A short length of dowel or metal used to hold stones securely while working them.

dopping The act of fastening a stone to a dopstick.

dopping wax A hard type of sealing wax used for dopping stones.

doublet A gemstone having a thin slice of different or self mineral cemented to its bottom surface for the purpose of strengthening or building up sufficient thickness to permit the gem to be used in a setting. A common method of making opal gems because of the value and rarity of the opal itself.

drum sander A machine with metal drums with an expandable covering of soft rubber, over which is slipped an abrasive belt of some kind, used in the finish sanding of gemstones before polishing.

druse The coating of small, projecting crystals on the surface of a rock or mineral; the crystalline lining of a geode. The adjective is "drusy."

enhydro A chalcedony or carnelian geode having the center cavity filled, or nearly filled, with water. The water may be many millions of years old, being the liquid left after the depositing of the minerals lining the cavity in the geode, which has not yet dissipated through the surrounding mineral.

gad; gadpoint A kind of prybar having either a chisel, pointed, or wedge-shaped end, usually with a boss on the opposite end against which a hammer can be struck. Used in the field for opening seams in rock.

geode A round, or nearly round, mass of mineral, hollow and lined with crystals of the same or another mineral, such as quartz or amethyst, formed by the filling of a bubble left in the rock when it was formed. In time, a geode would be filled completely, and then it would be called a nodule.

girdle The rim or outer edge of a gemstone at the base of a cabochon, and about one-third of the way down a faceted gemstone. The largest diameter.

indurated Hardened by the action of heat, pressure, or cementation, as in "indurated volcanic ash."

intaglio A gemstone in which the design is carved into the surface of the stone. The opposite of cameo.

intarsia The art of making pictures out of mineral pieces, putting them together on the same plane, much as assembling a jigsaw puzzle. The surface may then be ground true and polished.

labradorescence The chatoyant play of colors seen on the surface of the feldspar mineral labradorite. Some color is blue, some green, and some yellow. Certain specimens may show two or more of these colors simultaneously.

lap A plate of any substance upon which a gemstone is either ground to size and shape, sanded smooth, or polished. The plate is revolved either vertically or horizontally, the stone being held against the surface, upon which a coolant is constantly dripped while in operation.

magma The molten rock of the earth, held beneath the surface crust under great pressure. When forced to the surface, either as intrusive rock or in a volcanic eruption, it forms igneous rocks.

mammilary A series of concretions in minerals shaped something like breasts.

nodule A usually spherical or nearly spherical mass of mineral caused by the filling of a bubble formed in rock. Some nodules are irregularly shaped, and the size may vary from pea-size to enormous masses.

potch The name given to the base or matrix rock in which opal is found. Any poor-quality common material associated with opal.

Schiller flash The iridescent play of color upon the surface of labradorite feldspar.

septarium A concretionary nodule, usually of indurated clay or limestone, filled with other minerals, such as calcite, barite, etc.

sill The intrusion of magma into sedimentary rocks in a horizontal or nearly horizontal position.

slab A section of mineral sliced off an amorphous chunk of material; the first step in cutting gemstones from rough minerals.

traprock Any of the dark, fine-grained igneous rocks, especially basalt, occurring in large sheetlike masses.

triboluminescence The curious property of giving off light when rubbed or abraded.

tumbler A machine in which crushed bits of gem minerals are ground and polished by the rotation of a rubber-lined drum containing the stones, water, and abrasive or polishing grains.

vug A void or cavity in rock formations containing gem mineral deposits.

Index